SCOTTSDALE MEMORIES

PAUL R. MESSINGER

Library of Congress Cataloging Card Number pending.

Paul R. Messinger
Scottsdale Memories

Printed by Prisma Graphics, Phoenix, Arizona.

Photo credits

Burl Avery, Page 69

Kendall Carver, Pages 102, 103

City of Scottsdale/Scottsdale Public Library, Pages 7, 11, 37, 63, 73, 97

Helen Hughes, Page 51

Sue Jenkins, Page 47

Paul Messinger, Pages 15, 27, 29, 31, 35, 41, 45, 49, 63, 77, 83, 85, 89, 91, 99, 101

Charles Miller family, Page 17

National Park Service, Page 87

Phoenix College Sandprints 1950 Annual, Page 93

Scottsdale High School 1947 Annual, Page 55

Scottsdale High School 1948 Annual, Page 65

Scottsdale High School 1949 Annual, Pages 23, 39

Scottsdale Historical Society, Pages 3, 5, 9, 19, 21, 25, 33, 53, 57, 67, 79

© *Scottsdale Republic*, Nov. 11, 2005, photograph by Rob Schumacher. Used with
permission.   Permission does not imply endorsement. Page 59

Southwest Studio, Scottsdale Community College, Marshall Trimble, Page 13

Sue Witzeman, Page 53

This book is dedicated to my wife, Cora, with whom I've shared the many wonderful adventures of our lives.

Paul R. Messinger

TABLE OF CONTENTS

PREFACE

Stories about growing up in a small town never fail to evoke fond memories of a simpler time when we were young and there were no limits to our dreams.

Small towns are places where people can acquire a sense of security and familiarity. It's where people become better acquainted because there is more front porch sociability and sidewalk congeniality. It's a place where families spend more time socializing together, because there's not much else to do. And that's not necessarily a bad thing. Not too long ago, this description of a small town would have aptly described Scottsdale.

I grew up in a small town in northern Arizona. We used to say Ash Fork was so small that by the time the train pulled into town, it was already out of town. The same could have been said about Scottsdale had there been a railroad in town, which there wasn't.

I've always felt sorry for kids growing up in large cities. Sure, they have lots of amenities that can't be found in small towns, but they never get the chance to be so close to the great outdoors, drop their line in a fishing hole, ride horseback or go swimming in a creek on a warm summer day.

For the past several years, I've looked forward to reading Paul Messinger's bi-weekly columns in The *Scottsdale Republic*. He recounted memories of life in early-day Scottsdale. Many of them he experienced. And now he's consolidated some of his favorite columns into a book.

Reading one of Paul's stories conjures up images of a Norman Rockwell painting.

He tells wonderful tales of Scottsdale during a time when there was little traffic and no traffic lights. Most of the streets were unpaved roads where kids could still play marbles. Hitching posts still lined the storefronts on Scottsdale Road. The one high school was so small they played six-man football.

It's been said you know it's a small town if you could dial the wrong number on the telephone and wind up talking to somebody for half an hour anyway. Or, you could move to the other side of town and not have to fill out a change-of-address form at the post office. Everybody knew who the father of the pups was. And everyone knew whose checks were good and whose husbands weren't.

Scottsdale has changed from a small town of 400 people in the 1940s to a large city of a quarter million residents. Life was pretty simple back then, or so it seemed, and those are the kinds of stories Paul writes. He takes us on a happy trail ride down Memory Lane to those halcyon days. We can all take pride in our community's rich heritage thanks to Paul's wonderful stories.

Marshall Trimble
Official Arizona State Historian

3 MEN HELPED TURN LIGHTS ON FOR EARLY SCOTTSDALE

Scottsdale Republic, March 5, 2004

Today, we take everything for granted. But that wasn't the case in 1908, when the telephone first came to Scottsdale. Nor was it a decade later, when electricity had yet to arrive. The town's women were impatient. Their message was clear: "We want electricity now!"

E.O. Brown and Charles Miller (after whom today's Brown and Miller roads are named), along with W.E. Kimsey, took it upon themselves to contact the Salt River Valley Water Users Association (today's Salt River Project). They asked the "Water Users" to provide electricity.

The association didn't share the men's sense of urgency. Scottsdale was too small. Nonetheless, it offered to install a hydro-generator at Arizona Falls, a small "waterfall" across the Arizona Canal at 56th Street and Indian School Road. The overture was accepted. Brown, Miller and Kimsey formed a non-profit utility called Scottsdale Light and Power Co. It would purchase the electricity, distribute it and charge for what folks used.

The Water Users strung a 24,000-volt line from the generator to the downtown, using a network of transformers to reduce the voltage. The result was 25-cycle power.

For those who don't know, 25-cycle power is inferior to the 60-cycles we enjoy today. Instead of a steady stream of light, the soft glow continuously flickered. Still, any form of electricity was better than a smoky oil lamp.

When Scottsdale Light and Power began service, it had fewer than 150 customers. Kimsey served as secretary/treasurer of the utility until his son Mort took over the business in 1920. Mort Kimsey owned a gas station and repair garage at Scottsdale Road and Main Street. It was there, for 20 years, he collected the electric bills. By foot, bicycle, horseback and car, folks dropped off their payments.

In 1940, Scottsdale Light and Power was purchased by Central Arizona Light and Power Co. (known then as CALAPCO, today's Arizona Public Service Co.).

The CALAPCO strung new lines. The hydro-generator was abandoned. Scottsdale's electric service was upgraded to 60-cycles. Flickering lights were a thing of the past. Reading was a pleasure. Of course, everyone had to modify or replace their motors and electric appliances to accommodate the change. It was the price of progress. Few complained.

Mort Kimsey collected electricity payments at his gas station until his retirement. He was the fellow everyone knew. The Maricopa County Board of Supervisors appointed him to Scottsdale's first City Council. His colleagues subsequently selected him as Scottsdale's second mayor. Everywhere you looked, there was Mort.

From time to time, the Water Users and CALAPCO entered into "territorial" agreements. That specified which company would provide electricity where. Today, more than half a century later, APS (the old Scottsdale Light and Power Co. turned CALAPCO) still supplies electricity to downtown Scottsdale. Salt River Project (yesterday's Water Users) continues to supply electricity to the east.

Mort Kimsey's gas station and repair garage at Scottsdale Road and Main Street is where people paid their electric bills in the 1920s and '30s.

SHEEPHERDERS ONCE DROVE FLOCKS THROUGH SCOTTSDALE

Scottsdale Republic, March 26, 2004

When I look out my window at the thousands of cars passing through the intersection of Indian School and Miller roads, I think back 60 years to the mammoth sheep drives that used to pass this same way each spring and fall.

A few minutes before the sheep strode by, a man in a pickup truck would come through town honking his horn and shouting, "The sheep are coming!" Folks living alongside the road would rush into their yards.

Sometimes, if he wasn't in too big a rush, neighbors had a chance to ask him questions. Whose sheep were they? How many were there? Then, off he drove, down the road to warn others.

In those days, most of Arizona, including Scottsdale, was open range. It was each landowner's responsibility to protect his property from the approaching herd, not the sheepherders or the cattlemen. Whole families would stand along unfenced yards to make sure the sheep stayed in the roadway. Everyone worked together to keep one another's property safe.

Mind you, we're not talking about a handful of sheep taking a quiet Sunday stroll. Upward of 1,000 animals (maybe 2,000 or more) were involved, accompanied by two or three herdsmen and their herd dogs. They were joined by burros carrying camping gear and bed rolls.

Unlike cattlemen who rode horses, most sheepherders tended to their flocks on foot. They hiked a quarter to a third of the length of Arizona twice each year, spending their nights resting their feet under the stars. Their skilled dogs made sure the sheep stayed safely together, barking and nipping at their heels, corralling sheep that became separated from the main herd or lost their way.

It was a tremendous sight to see a herd of sheep a half a mile or more long, slowly moving past your farm as they headed toward Arizona's high country for summer or came back home for winter.

From Scottsdale, outbound for the summer, the herd made its way along the edge of the Salt River Indian Reservation and over the Evergreen Canal Bridge (a couple miles east of Pima Road). They traveled through the McDowell Mountain Pass, where the Mayo Clinic now sits, and along the base of the mountains east of Arizona 87. Then, they traversed Reno Pass near Sunflower and across the Tonto Basin to the cool pastures above the Sierra Anche Mountains.

While Scottsdale's dusty herds of yesteryear have given way to frustrating traffic jams, driving my SUV to and from work is still easier than driving just one sheep!

Huge herds of sheep, sometimes numbering between 1,000 and 2,000, clogged the streets in downtown Scottsdale twice a year as they headed to Arizona's high country for the summer and came back home for winter.

JUDGING BY THE SOUND OF IT, SCOTTSDALE'S ALL GROWN UP

Scottsdale Republic, April 23, 2004

The other day, a co-worker parked his car in an empty spot I was saving for a guest.

I called out to him, but he couldn't hear me. It was too noisy. Cars were speeding by. Airplanes were flying overhead. My voice was lost in the day-to-day drone of Indian School and Miller Roads.

As you can well imagine, Scottsdale was a whole lot quieter in the 1940s. Back then, we could call cattle as far as a quarter mile away. You could hear other farmers' voices even farther.

There were no televisions and few radios. People in the small Mexican community southeast of downtown Scottsdale often sang and played guitars. They were happy sounds that carried long distances at night, sounds we could all enjoy.

Likewise, when I was a young boy and we were cleaning the barn after milking, we would hear the Southern Pacific "Imperial" going through Tempe, some five miles away, at 5:30 in the morning. We also heard the "Golden State Limited" passing through at 10:30 each night.

We heard the rattle of the black iron bridge as trains crossed the Salt River and the sound of their whistles as they approached Rural Road. Sometimes, we could hear their faint whistles as far away as Mesa.

Drivers coming south on Scottsdale Road would slow down as they passed over the Arizona Canal, and then accelerate through the old downtown. Even though we lived almost a mile from the canal bridge, we could hear the clatter of its wooden planks as cars drove over.

I also remember the sounds of the Indian wagons heading home to the Salt River Reservation after a long day of shopping. We heard the horses' hoofs on the road and the rattle of the wooden wagon box as it passed by and slowly faded away.

Sometimes, the drivers would stop to talk. One family used to kid my dad about watering our lawn so he could mow it. They were stoic folks with a great sense of humor.

Today, you no longer hear the rooster's crow or the gobbling of herds of range turkeys. You hear the ring of cellphones instead.

Nor do you hear the moo of a cow or heifer giving birth, or the shrill call of the Dominguez family peacock announcing the approach of a stranger to their farm at Indian School and 82nd Street, known then as Dominguez Lane.

Things are different now. That's to be expected. Nonetheless, I miss those memorable sounds of time and place. Maybe you remember the quiet echoes of your own hometown.

Heading home after a day of shopping in Scottsdale, the Indian wagons resonated with the rattle of the wooden wagon boxes as they passed by local farms.

SCOTTSDALE GOT ITS NAME THROUGH NEWSPAPER ERROR

Scottsdale Republic, June 11, 2004

Albert G. Utley, a former Rhode Island banker, and his sister-in-law's brother William J. Murphy, the man who dug the Arizona Canal, owned 640 acres southeast of what we today call Indian School and Scottsdale Roads.

In 1894, he set aside 40 acres adjacent to that intersection to plat a new town.

On his plat, Utley laid out streets and specified all manner of detail, down to the actual lot sizes. Most were 40 feet wide and approximately 124 feet deep.

The eastern boundary of his "town" was today's Drinkwater Boulevard. The southern boundary was Garfield (today's Second Street). Other names he chose for the streets that ran east to west were Grant, Sherman and Sheridan. Years later, Grant would become First Avenue (or Pima Plaza). Sherman became Main Street. Sheridan was renamed First Street.

When he officially recorded his master plan with the Maricopa County Recorder, Utley decided to call his town Orangedale. The name was appropriate because the area was considered an ideal place to grow citrus.

Utley's town plat was across the road from a fellow named Winfield Scott, whose farm was known Valley-wide for its young citrus groves. Often, when Utley gave directions to his new town, he would refer to Scott's farm. It became the landmark that people used to find their way to Orangedale.

Not long after, Orangedale became the object of local media interest. And, in a fortuitous article published about it, the *Arizona Republican* (today's *Arizona Republic*) erroneously referred to Utley's "Orange"dale as "Scotts"dale.

Overnight, this minor mix-up tied Utley's tiny town to Winfield Scott, who was widely known for his willingness to experiment with new varieties of citrus and other plants. Ironically, that simple mistake did more to publicize the location of the new town than anything Utley had done to date.

Eventually, Utley amended his original filing with the Maricopa County Recorder and officially changed his town's name from Orangedale to Scottsdale. While there's no evidence that Scott and Utley ever discussed the name change, it's a foregone conclusion that Scott was honored to have the fledging town bear his name.

Today, you can find many of the businesses on Main Street, First Street and First Avenue sitting on the original lots drawn by Albert Utley more than 110 years ago. For example, Saba's Western Store stands on lot 18 of block 6. The Song family's Mexican Imports is on lot 14 of block 5.

The original 40-acre Scottsdale subdivision contained 208 lots. Today, the city of Scottsdale encompasses more than 180 square miles.

Originally known as Orangedale, the Arizona Republican (today's Arizona Republic) erroneously referred to the new town as Scottsdale in a newspaper article, assuming the town was named for Winfield Scott, a local farmer. The name was so popular it was formally adopted when Albert G. Utley officially filed the name with the Maricopa County Recorder's office.

'40s PAPERBOYS PEDALED PLENTY

Scottsdale Republic, June 25, 2004

In 1942, *The Arizona Republic* and *The Phoenix Gazette* were the only general circulation newspapers in what (back then) we called the Salt River Valley. *The Arizona Republic* (Arizona's "official" newspaper of record) covered the entire state, and *The Phoenix Gazette* covered greater Phoenix.

Subscribers who lived in Scottsdale received their newspapers courtesy of four carriers. Mind you, these were bicycle routes. And, at one time or another, I rode each one. My brother, Philip, cleaned our barn twice daily (after morning and evening milking) so I could deliver my newspapers.

Back then, we carried both the morning *Republic* and the evening *Gazette*, with the exception of Sunday. There was no evening newspaper on Sunday. As such, each route had to be ridden 13 times each week.

The routes were long. The "south" route (#489) was 21 miles. The "northwest" route (#477) lasted 11 miles. The "east" route (#478) was about 10 miles. The shortest route was five miles.

The routes ranged from 18 to 40 newspapers each. Oliver King was the head of circulation back then. Millan Leavett and (later on) Norman Wolf dropped off our newspapers each day for delivery.

In those days, because of the length of our routes and in the interest of time, we modified our bicycle gears so that a single turn of the pedals turned the rear tire four times. We could go really fast – on flat roads.

Given the length of the routes, the newspapers paid each carrier for the miles they rode (over and above the money we were paid to actually deliver the newspaper).

We got one dollar per mile per month. Therefore, an 11-mile route (ridden twice a day) paid $11 a month (plus 30 cents per newspaper subscription per month). The total pay for route No. 477 was, for example, $28 a month. A new bicycle, if you could get a wartime priority to buy one, generally cost $35 to $40. You do the math!

When I think back on my many paper routes over several years, I remember my mother sewing a pocket into my carrier bag. It was a holder for an atomizer filled with diluted ammonia to ward off dogs. A quick squirt kept me from being bitten. After they'd been sprayed a time or two, we could point our fingers at them, and they'd keep their distance.

I also remember how satisfying it was to watch the sunrise over Scottsdale's pristine desert and its gentle farm fields, or see coyotes coming home after a night's hunt. Nonetheless, it was lonely riding our bicycles down empty dirt roads in the early morning and late evening. Still, it gave one time to think.

Way back then, most every family in Scottsdale took one or both newspapers. And, over time, we got to know everyone in town.

Newspaper carriers in the early 1940s rode their bicycles 11 miles, twice a day, to deliver the morning and evening newspapers.

PAPAGO P.O.W. CAMP LIVED HARMONIOUSLY WITH VALLEY

Scottsdale Republic, July 30, 2004

The tail end of the 1930s saw the U.S. Army Cavalry leave today's Papago Park, where it had been headquartered for many years. World War II broke out soon thereafter.

During the war, from 1943 to 1945, hundreds of German and Italian prisoners were housed in barracks in a prisoner of war camp north of McDowell Road, east of the familiar Papago Buttes. High fences and barbed wire ran north, almost to Thomas Road.

Today, homes sit on the old prison site, along with some baseball fields, a blood bank and an Elks Lodge. The building used today by the Scottsdale Elks is one of the barracks that was used to house prisoners of World War II.

In general, the POWs and the community at-large got along well. Most of the prisoners, though not all, were non-commissioned men. They spent their days cleaning irrigation ditches for 10 cents an hour. The going rate was a dollar, but they got their room and board for free. Besides, how many prisoners of war were being paid anything?

One story that sticks out in my mind involved an unbroken pinto horse belonging to the William Schrader family. One day, a truckload of prisoners were clearing an irrigation ditch near what was known as Schrader's Pond.

A German prisoner spotted the pinto horse asleep, standing beside a fence. When no one was looking, he scaled the fence, planning to take a joy ride. The surprised horse had other ideas. It began bucking wildly before running into a thicket of mesquite.

When the hapless prisoner emerged, his shirt was torn, and his arms and legs were bleeding from dozens of minor scratches and scrapes. The guard took the injured man to the nearby Schrader house, where Mrs. Schrader generously offered to clean his wounds.

When she was done, he was as good as new. Everyone had a good laugh.

While for most POWs it was irrigation ditches by day, for all POWs it was motion pictures by night. The prison camp had an auditorium where inmates were shown American movies. Walter Jennings, a civilian guard, would let me and my friend, Willie Duncan, sit in the back of the theater on show nights. It was me, Willie, and a room full of prisoners.

As I think back today, I wonder whether similar POW camps elsewhere operated in such harmony. The only exception was a brief escape by a cadre of German U-boat officers on Christmas Eve. Every one of them was recaptured.

After the war ended, the camp became a Veterans Administration hospital, where hundreds of soldiers received care. During my college years as an *Arizona Republic* auto driver who delivered bundles of newspapers to an army of young carriers in the East Valley, I finished my route by going room to room at the "Papago" VA Hospital selling newspapers to the wounded GIs.

The hospital eventually was moved to Seventh Street and Indian School Road in Phoenix (now the Carl T. Hayden VA Medical Center). And several decades later (in the 1990s), a small group of former German prisoners (then in their 70s and 80s) traveled back to Scottsdale to reminisce over days gone by.

By the time they arrived, only a couple of the original buildings remained. I was fortunate to meet some of these men on the occasion of their first and only return visit to the site of the Scottsdale POW camp they once called home.

During the war, from 1943 to 1945, hundreds of German and Italian prisoners were housed in barracks at Camp Papago, a prisoner of war camp south of Thomas Road, east of the familiar Papago Buttes.

SCC GREW FROM SCOTTSDALE CIVIC LEADERS' DREAM, EFFORT

Scottsdale Republic, August 27, 2004

In the spring of 1966, Scottsdale Mayor Bud Tims met with several local business people to gauge their support for the construction of a community college in Scottsdale. It was apparent most folks felt that Scottsdale was ripe for a college campus.

Although the proposed campus would, at least initially, have a smaller population from which to draw (compared with colleges elsewhere), the city was experiencing rapid growth. The challenge was gaining the approval of the community college governing board.

Meanwhile, the Scottsdale City Council and City Manager Bill Donaldson had begun to establish several volunteer committees. They were called "STEP" committees, which stood for Scottsdale Town Enrichment Programs.

One STEP committee was formed to look at parks. What kinds of recreational spaces were other communities building? What kind of park system should Scottsdale build?

Other STEP committees focused on everything from sewers and traffic to roads and the proposed construction of a new city hall. It was only natural to form a STEP committee to secure a community college.

I was one of the people who talked with Tims about the need for a college. Subsequently, I guess I must have missed a meeting, because before I knew it, I was appointed chairman of the community college STEP committee. I served alongside Billie Gentry and 12 others.

Our first order of business was to invite Bill Van Loo, a member of the community college governing board who represented our part of the county. He advised us to attend the regular board meetings, which we did for two years.

At every meeting, we asked the board to consider Scottsdale as the site of its next college campus. We explained why we thought Scottsdale was a prime location. Dr. John Prince, district chancellor at the time, gave monthly reports to the board on our long-standing request. And, in 1968, he presented several site options (including the leasing of 160 acres from the Salt River Indian Community). He also agreed to begin offering evening college classes in 1969 at Scottsdale High School (which has since been torn down).

Not long afterward, the board forwarded a $14 million bond package to county voters, with $4 million of that earmarked to build a Scottsdale community college. The bonds would pay for the construction of permanent classrooms, a science complex and a library, as well as the movement of temporary classroom buildings onto the campus site. Other proceeds would benefit community colleges in Mesa, Glendale and Phoenix.

Leonard Huck (of Valley National Bank) was appointed general chairman of the county bond committee. I was asked to lead the Scottsdale campaign committee. Our job was to urge Scottsdale voters to approve the entire bond package. The voters said "yes," and the result is the community college you see on the north side of Chaparral Road, east of Loop 101. Classes began there in 1970.

Today, Scottsdale is one of several community colleges in Maricopa County. Together, they make up the largest community college system in the country.

14

With dogged determination, Scottsdale leaders in the 1960s convinced the Maricopa County Community College District to build Scottsdale Community College, which opened in 1970. Here, community leaders gathered for the college's groundbreaking.

CITY JUST MISSED HAVING OWN INTER-URBAN RAILROAD

Scottsdale Republic, September 10, 2004

An old friend and former railroader recently chided me because Scottsdale doesn't have – and never has had – a railroad. Not one foot of track has ever been laid. Not one boxcar has ever rolled through town.

As such, he opined that I'd never be able to write a "Scottsdale" story about a railroad. I reflected on his challenge, thought back over several years and concluded he was wrong.

In 1905, two stagecoach lines began offering competing services between Phoenix and Scottsdale, and the demand for their services increased. By 1909, Winfield Scott (after whom Scottsdale was named) and others began to solicit monetary pledges to underwrite the cost of establishing a gasoline-powered, inter-urban trolley. It would do what the stage lines were doing, only better, and serve the transportation needs of the area's annual influx of winter visitors.

As it was envisioned at the time, the initial tracks would have extended east from Phoenix along McDowell Road to 48th Street, then turned north to Indian School Road, and then east again to Scottsdale.

To further his ambitious dream, Scott purchased five acres of land in Scottsdale. It was there that a terminal would be built, leaving sufficient room to "turn the trolley car around" for its return trip to Phoenix, and its anticipated arrival at what would soon become the new Ingleside Inn (which was under construction two miles west of Scottsdale). It also would serve businesses and other resorts, not to mention nearby residents.

The Ingleside Inn operated for almost 40 years before it was converted, in the mid-1940s, into a private school for girls called Brownmoor. The school closed several years later, the result of redevelopment pressures reflecting increasing real estate values. The Ingleside Golf Course became today's Arizona Country Club.

Funding for the trolley was solicited from the property owners along its proposed route. About half of the $125,000 it was estimated that it would cost to build the system was pledged within weeks. Scott and his partners concluded their idea was a feasible one. They decided their trolley line would be called the Orangebelt and Scottsdale Railroad.

To further improve its chances of success, they planned to extend the trolley's tracks south to Tempe and Mesa and, eventually, west to Glendale. Their tracks would link together the communities of the Salt River Valley. Furthermore, they could be used by Valley farmers to haul sugar beets from farms in the East Valley to the Southwest Sugar Beet Co. in Glendale for processing into sugar.

The members of the board of directors of the Orangebelt and Scottsdale Railroad were its president, Winfield Scott, its vice-president, L.J. Rice and Charles Miller (after whom Miller Road eventually was named), as well as Frank Alkire and N.A. Morford.

Unfortunately for my aforementioned friend and the rest of us who might have been served by such a "Scottsdale" railroad, the project never got off the ground. Scott's death one year into its planning probably is the primary reason nothing further happened.

Nonetheless, those of us who live in Scottsdale can take pride in the fact that a century ago those who founded this community tried to establish a privately financed transportation system that, had it been built, might still be serving Scottsdale and the rest of the Valley today.

It's interesting to note that almost 100 years later, another effort is underway to connect the Valley's disparate communities with a modern (and publicly financed) "trolley" system called light rail. It remains to be seen whether its tracks ever will extend into Scottsdale.

I've often thought it unique that Scottsdale became the Valley's principal "end destination" point for tourists without benefit of a passenger airport, a railroad or, until 2001, an official state or federal highway within or touching its borders.

In the early 1900s, a group known as the Orangebelt and Scottsdale Railroad company envisioned starting a trolley service in Scottsdale. It never happened and Scottsdale has never had a rail service of any kind in the city. Pictured here is Charles Miller, one of the company's directors, with his wife Daisy, daughter Murle and son Bill. Miller Road is named for Charles Miller.

17

AIRPORT HAD ITS ORIGINS AS BASE TO TRAIN WWII PILOTS

Scottsdale Republic, September 24, 2004

War was on the horizon in 1940 and the federal government was getting ready to wage it.

Hitler had our attention. We had no inkling of what was to come at Pearl Harbor. Preparation for war was the prudent thing to do, and Arizona's wide-open skies made it an ideal place to teach young combat pilots to fly.

A number of potential training sites were identified throughout the Valley, and three of them finally were chosen - Thunderbird Field in Glendale, Thunderbird II in Scottsdale and Falcon Field in Mesa.

It was decided that Thunderbird II would be built on the northeastern corner of what is now Thunderbird and Scottsdale Roads. By the time construction was complete, the United States had entered World War II. What was then known as Southwest Airways, under contract to the federal government, operated all three pilot training facilities.

At the beginning of the war, few instructors and airplanes were available for pilot training. To bridge this shortage (until the nation's factories could manufacture a sufficient number of training aircraft and enough instructors could be trained), the government organized a local fleet of civilian aircraft. Each plane's owner-pilot was put to work training Arizona's first class of pilot cadets.

As such, every type of single-engine airplane available could be seen flying over the practice areas surrounding Scottsdale. Some of the planes had been built in the early 1930s. Others were newer, having been built right up to the war years.

Men like Lee Moore, owner of A.L. Moore & Sons Mortuary in Phoenix, would get to the airport each day at sunrise and fly until mid-morning. Then he went to work until 3 or 4 p.m., only to return to Thunderbird II to teach student pilots until dark.

Malcolm White, a deputy sheriff and owner of White's Café and Bar in Scottsdale, did the same thing. Later, he became Scottsdale's first mayor and a partner in Collar, Williams and White Engineers.

Others who gave their time to Thunderbird II included Dorothy Cavalliere Ketchum Roberts, who volunteered her time as a parachute rigger. She became Scottsdale's second town clerk. Lucy Lutes was one of the first women certified as an aircraft mechanic.

When the first training planes began arriving, the "borrowed" civilian aircraft were returned and many were retired, as they had been flown 12 to 16 hours a day. Such intensive use had taken a significant toll on engines and airframes.

After the war, many of the 5,500 pilots who were trained at Thunderbird II came back to live in Arizona. The airport itself was used by Arizona State University until it was sold to the Seventh-day Adventist Church, which operated a day school and boarding high school on the site. In 1967, the runways and taxiways became Scottsdale Municipal Airport. The Seventh-day Adventist Church hired George Tewksbury to initiate the development that is now called Scottsdale Airpark. Bill Arthur (chairman of the first airport commission), the City of Scottsdale and others with an interest in the airpark continued its development.

Today, the airport and the business and industrial park surrounding it are considered world-class.

What we know today as Scottsdale Airport started in the 1940s as a training site for WWII pilots. Many local area pilots devoted their time and airplanes to the effort. When Thunderbird II closed in October 1944, 5,500 pilots had been trained here in Scottsdale.

STORM SENT FLOOD ACROSS VALLEY

Scottsdale Republic, October 15, 2004

In June 1943, we had a very hard rain. It started during the night and came in pounding waves. There would be 10 or 15 minutes of driving rain, followed by gentle showers. Then the rain would start coming down hard again.

This went on for several hours, beginning around 3 a.m. and lasting past 7 a.m. The ground eventually became waterlogged, and all of the low areas filled with runoff from the storm. It was the biggest rain I had ever seen.

I wore my slicker on my newspaper route that day. My travels took me south to Curry Road, then east over to Hayden Road, up to McDowell Road, then farther east to the Salt River Indian Agency near Alma School Road.

Coming back toward Scottsdale, near Thomas and Pima Roads, I ran into a broad, but shallow, stream of water. It probably was 75 yards wide and flowing fairly quickly. I gave my bike a good run of speed before hitting the edge of the water. I almost got clear across when, all of a sudden, I found myself mired in water 2 feet deep.

The force of the water forced me off my bike, and I ended up dragging it and my bag full of newspapers to the far side of what today is called the 86th Street Wash. I wasn't scared. But there's no denying I was surprised by the speed and depth of the water. Wet newspapers ended up in the mailboxes of my next three subscribers.

As it turned out, the water had only begun to run. By mid-morning, it was flowing fast and furious down the Indian Bend Wash. It ran from bank to bank, overrunning what is now the Bashas' shopping center at Indian School and Hayden roads, and west to the old Schrader home at what is now 78th Street. In fact, the Schraders had built a dirt berm around their home to keep floodwaters at bay.

Since it was summer and school was out, a lot of people, young and old, came down to the water's edge at Indian School, Thomas and McDowell Roads (the only paved streets that led to Indian Bend Wash) to see the floodwaters rush by. Later that day, we saw a five-room frame house belonging to Dick Searls float past us, still intact.

By the next day, the floodwaters had receded to a trickle. Barbed-wire fences were wrapped around trees. Many of the row crops that had been planned for silage or vegetable harvest were lost. In contrast, the hay and alfalfa fields came back quickly and produced a bountiful yield that year.

According to that day's *Arizona Republic*, there had been 28 breaks in the Arizona Canal. Homes were flooded. The state Capitol on Washington Street had been sandbagged to protect it from the flood. In Scottsdale and east Phoenix, the water had run off Camelback Mountain, washed out nearby canals and flooded the farmland below.

Although the flood did a lot of damage, no lives were lost. Of course, there were a lot fewer people living in the area way back then. And, in contrast to today, those who lived here then assumed their own losses.

Landowners did what they could to protect themselves and their property, and they helped their neighbors to the extent that they could. Folks didn't look to the government for anything. They just got back to normal on their own.

I was 13 back then. The big flood, and how people reacted to it, left quite an impression on me.

Water flowing down Indian Bend Wash after heavy rains used to cause extensive flooding in Scottsdale. As a lad of 13 delivering newspapers in 1943, Paul Messinger and his bicycle got caught in the beginnings of a flood that ran from bank to bank, overrunning what is now the Bashas' shopping center at Indian School and Hayden roads, and west to the old Schrader home at what is now 78th Street.

MELON-PATCH JOBS TESTED CHARACTER OF VALLEY BOYS

Scottsdale Republic, October 29, 2004

C.B. Reddell lived where Miller Road and Main Street now meet. He owned 40 acres where Scottsdale City Hall and our main library stand today. From 1944 to 1949, he planted watermelons on that land. Many of the high school boys of that era, as well as Reddell's boys, worked part of their summer harvesting those melons, starting around June 20 and lasting through the end of July.

Besides his 40 acres, Reddell also planted melons on my dad's south 10 acres (where Our Lady of Perpetual Help Church subsequently was built) and the 80 acres where Bashas' Markets Inc. has a store at Indian School and Hayden Roads, extending south to Osborn Road, where Scottsdale Presbyterian Church and many Hallcraft homes now sit.

Along Hayden, each row was a half-mile long. When we were turning vines or tossing melons to the field trailer, those rows seemed endless. There was no shade. A hat was our only protection from the sun. During the harvest, we worked seven days a week, 12 hours each day. The grueling schedule was a good test of character. The pay seemed good, too – 50 cents per hour often amounted to $50 or $60 a week.

Other farms where melons were raised included Mike Dominguez (40 acres between 82nd Street and Granite Reef Road along Indian School Road) and Mrs. George Borg's 40 acres south of her home (between Camelback Road and what was the Casa Blanca Inn).

The melons were planted on a 6-foot-wide strip of land, with an irrigation furrow on each side. This provided enough water for the plant while keeping it and the maturing melons out of the water. Every 12th row would be 13 feet wide, creating a lane for the small tractors to pull the wagons used to haul the melons from the fields. They took the melons to market in places like Kansas City, Los Angeles, Salt Lake City and Denver.

About daylight each harvest morning, one or two men would cut the ripe melons from their vines. A young man followed each picker and would put the melons on the edge of each 6-foot row. Because melons don't ripen at the same time, the picking was repeated every few days until the harvest was done.

It took six high school boys to load the field trailers, plus a stacker on the trailer and the tractor driver. The melons were tossed from boy to boy until they got to the wagon. Then the biggest (or the strongest) boy would toss the melons up to the stacker on the wagon.

We usually had two tractors pulling wagons, so as soon as we finished loading one wagon, the other one was already returning from the lot where the big-rig trucks were loaded.

We prided ourselves on always catching each melon tossed to us. However, as hard as we tried, few of us could go an entire summer without dropping and breaking a melon. It was hard work. We handled upward of 60 tons of melons a day.

The melons we harvested were Klondikes or Peacock Klondikes. They were beautiful green melons with white bellies. Grade-A melons weighed 18 to 22 pounds, each with a uniform shape. While loading the big truck, we culled out the melons that didn't meet that standard. The smaller melons tasted just as good and were sold locally.

Today, when I do the math, I'm amazed that these fields produced more than 3,000 tons of melons each season. It's hard to believe that a small vine, with proper water, fertilizer and sunlight, could produce that much melon in just a few short weeks.

A lot of folks owe their strong backs to each summer's watermelon harvest. They include Albert Owens, Bill Stone, John Stone, Billy Williams, Willie Duncan and the Thomases and Brockemontys from the Salt River Indian Reservation. I harvested melons for four summers.

C.B. Reddell was a local Scottsdale farmer who annually planted many acres of melons on land that is now occupied by Scottsdale City Hall, the main library and Our Lady of Perpetual Help Church. These fields, which were harvested by local boys working tirelessly every summer, yielded as much as 60 tons of melons a day, totaling more than 3,000 tons of melons per season.

MIGHTY SCHOOL DISTRICT GREW FROM HUMBLEST BEGINNINGS

Scottsdale Republic, November 12, 2004

During the winter of 1895-96, Alza Blount taught school, specifically her children and some of her neighbors' children, in her home. The house was on Second Street, where the Scottsdale Police Department sits today.

During that same winter, several new families moved to Scottsdale. The Underhills came from New York. The Ruhls traveled from Kansas City. The Rosses arrived from Minneapolis. The Wards moved from Chicago. The Rev. Banks' family left Toledo, Ohio, for Arizona. Each of these families had children. The need for a real school was paramount.

On June 30, 1896, Winfield Scott (after whom Scottsdale is named) and several of his neighbors prepared and signed a petition requesting the establishment of a Scottsdale school district.

C.W. Crouse, the Maricopa County School superintendent, accepted the petition.

On July 13, 1896, the Maricopa County Board of Supervisors formally voted to authorize the formation of Scottsdale School District 48. Winfield Scott, John Tait and Frank Titus were appointed to serve on the district's first school board.

All that was missing was a school, a teacher and the money to pay for both. The funds needed to operate the district eventually would come from local property taxes. They wouldn't be available until the following year, because the current year's budget was already closed.

Being the resourceful folks they were, they decided not to wait.

They gathered what few dollars they could from Maricopa County and then dug into their own pockets to raise enough money to build a modest wooden school.

That September, with tools, lumber and all manner of building materials in hand, the locals built Scottsdale's first schoolhouse. It was on the south side of Main Street, a few hundred feet east of Brown. They completed the building, with the exception of some window details, in time for a picnic later that day. The next day, Sunday, church services were held in the new school building. It must have been pretty crowded, because the building was only 16 feet by 18 feet (288 square feet) in size.

Alza Blount volunteered to teach classes in the new school. She did so until funds were found to pay the salary of a permanent teacher to replace her.

By 1909, the district was serving 32 students. In anticipation of growth, a larger red brick schoolhouse was built to replace the old wooden schoolhouse. It was dedicated on February 26, 1910.

Luminaries such as Thomas Riley Marshall (who later became vice-president of the United States under Woodrow Wilson) and Richard Sloan (Arizona's territorial governor) spoke at the building's dedication. The building had two classrooms and a full basement, which also served as an auditorium. Today, the Red Brick School House is now the home of the Scottsdale Historical Society.

In 1923, Scottsdale's first high school opened a few blocks away on a 10-acre site on the north side of Indian School Road.

In 1928, Scottsdale Grammar School opened at Second Street and Marshall. In the 1950s, it was renamed Loloma School.

Scottsdale's original wooden schoolhouse and a small ancillary building adjacent to it were removed in the 1940s to make room for more playground space at the Red Brick School House. By that time, it had been named Coronado School.

Years later, in 1954, that school was closed and its name transferred to the newly completed Coronado High School at Miller Road and Oak Street.

Over a period of 114 years, and from the most humble of beginnings, a huge school district has grown.

In September of 1896, with tools, lumber and all manner of building materials in hand, Scottsdale locals built the town's first schoolhouse. It was on the south side of Main Street, a few hundred feet east of Brown.

3 MORE RAILROAD TALES SURE TO RAISE YOUR EYEBROWS

Scottsdale Republic, December 10, 2004

A few months ago, I wrote about the Orangebelt and Scottsdale Railroad. Since then, three more railroad stories have come to mind.

The first occurred in the mid-1940s, when I severely bent the bumper on my dad's 1937 International pickup truck. A family friend, Ivy Avery, owned a gas station at Thomas and Scottsdale Roads (where the McDonald's restaurant stands today).

He suggested that I drive the truck to a railroad siding, chain the truck's bumper to the railroad track, and use hydraulic jacks to spring the bumper back into its original shape. The railroad track wouldn't bend. The bumper would have to. That sounded great.

My friend, Willie Duncan, and I gathered the needed items and drove from Scottsdale (which had no railroad tracks) to Tempe (which did). We parked the truck right on the track just off what was then called Transmission Road (near where Arizona State University's Sun Devil Stadium sits today).

We chained the front bumper of my dad's truck to the track. And, within a few minutes, our hydraulic jacks had bent the bumper back like new. Ivy Avery's idea had worked.

About that time, we felt the vibrations of a train on the track to which we had chained dad's truck. Not good. Believe me, you never saw two boys unchain a truck bumper from a railroad track with greater efficiency than we did that day.

Willie jumped into the truck and backed it out of harm's way. About 20 seconds later, the train passed by without incident. I never straightened a bumper like that again, even though I've bent a few since.

My next story takes me back to 1962, when my wife, Cora, and I drove from Scottsdale down the west coast of Mexico. Along the way, we found out that the Culican River had washed away the highway bridge.

There was a handmade sign in Spanish indicating a detour to a railroad bridge about a half-mile away. The river was wide, and the railroad bridge was almost a mile long. Next to the bridge was a small building. Two men came out and approached our car.

They wanted five pesos to cross the bridge. Since they didn't look official, I questioned why I had to pay to cross. After a few minutes of mixed Spanish and English, we finally understood the reason for the payment.

You could cross the railroad trestle for free, if you wanted. But, if you paid, they would tell you when the train was coming. Needless to say, we paid then and again 10 days later on our way back to Scottsdale.

Speaking of bridges, there's a story that the late Harold McBurney used to tell about his friend, Charley M. Lewis. It seems Charley had saved up enough money to purchase a small motorcycle. One day, while he was riding, he decided to take a shortcut across the Salt River and rode his motorcycle over the railroad bridge just north of downtown Tempe.

About halfway across the bridge, he saw a freight train rounding the curve and coming over the bridge. Poor Charley. He barely had time to climb out on to the concrete piers holding up the bridge and pull his motorcycle after him.

There Charley stood, holding onto his motorcycle with one hand and the trembling bridge with his other hand while the train passed by. It was a long train, and Charley feared he couldn't hold on to the bridge, much less his motorcycle, much longer.

As we all know, fear often is a great motivator. And, in the end, Charley was able to hold on to both.

As the train trundled into the distance, and mustering what strength he had left, Charley pulled himself and his motorcycle back on to the bridge and continued to cross it.

As Charley had so amply demonstrated, workin' on the railroad was one thing. Hangin' off a railroad bridge was quite another.

Artist Harold McBurney's depiction of Charley M. Lewis' memorable motorcycle ride across the Salt River on the railroad bridge just north of downtown Tempe. About halfway across the bridge, Charley was confronted with a freight train. Charley climbed onto one of the bridge's concrete piers, holding onto the bridge for dear life with one hand while holding onto his motorcycle with his other hand. He survived.

TALE OF AMBULANCE SERVICE

Scottsdale Republic, January 7, 2005

In the mid-1950s, Walker McCune, a retired lumber mogul living on the southwestern corner of 56th Street and east Thomas Road, witnessed an automobile accident in north Scottsdale.

He called the police and an ambulance, the latter taking an hour to arrive. The delay and the suffering resulting from it bothered McCune. A man of action, he offered to donate a van and the gear needed to equip an ambulance. In return, Scottsdale volunteers agreed to staff it.

The volunteers were trained to provide emergency care and to transport injured patients to Valley hospitals. The van (Scottsdale's "first" ambulance) was kept in Jack and Ruth McMahon's backyard near First Street and Hinton. Jack rode the ambulance. Ruth rounded up the volunteers. The responsiveness of the service was hampered by the time it took to field a crew.

In 1958, my wife, Cora, and I decided to establish a mortuary on the southeastern corner of Miller and Indian School Roads, the site of my parent's dairy farm. In order to get our proposed building inspected to the satisfaction of state regulators, we needed to annex ourselves into Scottsdale, which at the time was less than one square mile. Our property was accepted as one of the city's first annexations.

Soon after, we applied for a use permit to operate our mortuary. A public hearing was held to consider our request. Scottsdale Mayor Mort Kimsey, chairman of the meeting, asked if we were going to provide ambulance services. We told him no.

"Then, I guess this hearing is over," he said. But before he brought down his gavel, he suggested tabling our request so that we could reconsider our position.

Two weeks later, when we returned to present our case, ambulance services were included in our proposal. Our use permit was granted. We got a mortuary, and the city got an ambulance service, its second.

Although I had accumulated five years of ambulance experience during my previous eight years in the funeral business, it wasn't something I enjoyed. Nonetheless, we stretched our finances and purchased a modern ambulance.

We bought everything needed to provide first-class service. When we started, ambulance calls cost $7.50 each, rising to $10 in 1960. Still, even with 250 calls a month, we lost money. Something had to be done to stem the tide of red ink. We decided to expand our service, increasing the number of vehicles and support staff and bidding for contracts.

It wasn't long before we were serving the Valley's automobile and motorcycle racetracks, ongoing product testing by tire manufacturers and the Arizona State Fair. It was a profitable strategy at a time when our mortuary was barely making ends meet.

We operated the ambulance franchise for 10 years, 24 hours a day, 7 days a week. Cora coordinated calls for service while the rest of us went on the road. We responded to at least one late-night call each day. Sometimes, there were as many as five or six calls in a night.

In 1958, when Paul and Cora Messinger applied to the City of Scottsdale for a permit to operate a mortuary in the city, then Mayor Mort Kimsey made it clear they would also have to operate an ambulance service. The mortuary operated the ambulance for 10 years, 24 hours a day, seven days a week. This was their first ambulance.

In 1968, Homer Johnston, a fellow with ambulance experience, came to town. He wanted to start an ambulance business. Unfortunately, he had no money.

By that time (and like me), David Hawkins of Green Acres Mortuary, Lawrence and Ed Carr of the Carr Mortuary and Tempe Mortuary wanted out of their ambulance businesses, too. Each of us gave Homer our vehicles or ambulance equipment and $4,000. We supported his franchise application.

The cities of Scottsdale and Tempe didn't share our enthusiasm. Homer would have to succeed for two years, or we wouldn't be permitted to abandon our respective ambulance responsibilities. To make sure Homer succeeded, we anted up more cash.

Homer and his Buena Vista Ambulance Service made it through the two-year trial period. Soon after, Bill Kordsman of Tucson bought Homer's ambulance franchise. Kord's Ambulance would take over Buena Vista Ambulance.

Now, decades later, the original Messinger Arizona Ambulance franchise is operating as Robert Ramsey's P.M.T. Ambulance Service, which is still operational today.

OLDER FOLKS PASSED ON MEMORIES NOW VIEWED AS HISTORY

Scottsdale Republic, February 18, 2005

When I was growing up in Scottsdale in the 1930s and '40s, there were a lot of older folks in my life who knew firsthand about events that today occurred anywhere from 100 to 140 years ago.

I have a clear memory of several of them.

My grandfather, Henry Messinger, was born in 1859. He used to tell me stories about families that had lost sons during the Civil War. He described the shock and anger at President Abraham Lincoln's assassination.

My grandfather lived in a little farming town called Fulton, in northern Indiana. He was a butcher during the winter and a farmer and barn-builder during the summer.

During the cold months, he traveled from farm to farm butchering hogs and cows. He would cut the steaks and roasts and help can the meat that wasn't going to be eaten before the spring thaw.

In return, he received one-fourth of what he butchered (and sometimes the hide). He would sell his share of the meat from a small building downtown on Wednesdays and Saturdays. Occasionally, the owner of the animal that my grandfather butchered would ask him to sell their share of the meat as well. He would post signs in the window of his store telling customers what kind of meat he would have for sale and when he would have it, based on his butchering contracts.

My grandfather also made oak pins during the winter. They were pieces of wood that were 1½ to 2 inches in diameter and 18 inches long.

They were shaved until they were round and tapered. He would put them in baskets next to his fireplace to dry them out. Those pins would be used for barn-building come summer. Holes were drilled in the big timbers that were used to frame the huge panels that formed the barn walls. When the panels were finished, they were stood erect. Then, my grandfather would climb up a ladder and drive the oak pins through the holes in the giant timbers in order to hold the side panels of the barn together.

Over time, the dry pins would take on moisture and expand to the point that they never would come out of the holes. As recently as 2001, I saw one of the barns that my grandfather built in 1914. It was still standing strong after all these many years.

My other grandfather, Louis Felder, was the local druggist in Fulton. He learned his trade working for the Baxter Drug Store in Rochester, Indiana, about nine miles away.

The people at Baxter's taught him how to gather roots, herbs and tree bark. He learned about the healing powers of honey and sulfur, as well as the various acids and other elements that were used in a pharmacy.

Years later, he taught me the ingredients for aspirin and told me how he used to make aspirin pills by hand. He ran his drugstore from 1899 until he suffered a stroke in his store in 1947. He died the next day.

My mother used to tell me stories about the young men from Fulton who traveled south to dig the Panama Canal. Several of them died on the job. Others returned home, only to die of malaria or other jungle diseases. She knew all of their names and often wondered what they might have accomplished in life had they lived.

A few weeks ago, my wife, Cora, and I passed through the Panama Canal. It was a magnificent thing to see. It turns out that the French lost 22,000 men in their unsuccessful attempt to build the canal. A quarter of a century later, America lost several hundred more before the canal was finished.

Fulton, Indiana and the Panama Canal are a long way from Scottsdale. But my memories of the stories told to me by my parents and grandparents are as fresh today as they were when I first heard them.

Grandfather Henry Messinger and Great Aunt Mary Elizabeth Messinger Richardson pictured in front of the Messinger family home built in Indiana in the 1850s. Grandfather Messinger, pictured on his horse, told Paul Messinger stories about the Civil War, including the shock and anger he felt at President Abraham Lincoln's assassination.

DESPITE HUMBLE ORIGIN, SCOTTSDALE KEPT EYES ON FUTURE

Scottsdale Republic, March 4, 2005

When Scottsdale petitioned for incorporation in 1951, it wasn't fully prepared to operate as an actual city, which is normal when most cities initially incorporate. The members of the Maricopa County Board of Supervisors accepted the petitions, oversaw the incorporation process and appointed Scottsdale's first City Council.

The five council members they appointed were Malcolm White (who later became Mayor), Bill Miller, Mort Kimsey, Jack Sweeney and E.G. Scott. Miller resigned shortly after his appointment, and George Cavalliere took his place. The City Council was expanded to seven members in 1952, when John Shoeman and Jim Frederick took their seats alongside the rest.

Among their first tasks was the selection of a town clerk, a city attorney and a treasurer. They also contacted Lou Witzeman, the founder of Rural/Metro Fire Department. Through Lou, they arranged for citywide fire protection for $4,260 for the first year.

Lou also made the breakroom at the fire station available for City Council meetings. It was 300 to 400 square feet in size and functioned as Scottsdale's first City Council chambers.

Vergie Lutes Brown became the first town clerk. She was followed by Dorothy Cavalliere Ketchum Roberts who held the post for many years. Don Baumann was Scottsdale's first city attorney, followed by my brother, Philip "William" Messinger, in 1958. George Song followed Phil.

In 1954, the original Coronado School (previously known as the Red Brick School House) was closed. The vacant building became Scottsdale's second City Hall. The building was roughly 2,000 square feet. The Police Department headquarters was in the basement.

Public hearings regarding my family's petition to annex 10 acres of our farm into Scottsdale, and our subsequent zoning application to build our first mortuary, were held in that building in the summer of 1958.

Not long afterward, an addition was built on the west side of the school building (aka City Hall). This enabled most of the Police Department to move out of the basement. A small jail was added, along with some general city office space. The new addition also included Scottsdale's first "real" City Council chambers.

By the early 1960s, Scottsdale's burgeoning city staff had outgrown both the school building and the addition. In order to provide much-needed office and work space, a deal was struck with an outfit called Butler Homes. They agreed to rent to the city the lion's share of a new, two-story retail office building. This became Scottsdale's third City Hall, and remained so until 1968, when the City began construction of its current City Hall complex.

Its design was called contemporary Sonoran, a concept pioneered by Bennie Gonzales. The exterior was massive in appearance, with deeply set windows and doors. Inside, the building was open, with differing departments seamlessly blending into one another. There were few doors or walls. The ceiling contained several stained glass windows.

The focal point of the building was, and

remains, its "Kiva" or main City Council chamber. Unfortunately, in recent years (and for security reasons), much of the building's original openness has given way to doors, walls and other barriers, the effect of which has been to eliminate a lot of open space to the public. The original design concept was both unique and citizen-friendly. Those, of course, were different times.

Submerging Civic Center Boulevard (now Drinkwater Boulevard) and building the beautiful civic center mall adjacent to it that we enjoy today was begun in the mid-1970s. It took an entire decade to complete the project.

Despite all of the moves from one set of temporary offices to another over the better part of 20 years, council members and city staffers kept their eyes focused on Scottsdale's future. And, when you consider all that's happened to Scottsdale during these past many years, thank goodness they did.

Scottsdale was incorporated as a city in 1951. Pictured here is one of the early City Councils, along with two staff members.

From left, George "Doc" Cavalliere, Jack Sweeney, City Attorney Philip Messinger, John Shoeman, City Clerk Dorothy Cavalliere Ketchum Roberts, Mayor Malcolm White, E.G. Scott, Mort Kimsey and Lute Wasbotten.

PICKING UP VALUABLE LESSON ON FRIGID NIGHT IN '48 DODGE

Scottsdale Republic, March 18, 2005

In the fall of 1948, my friend Albert Owens and I were hired by *The Arizona Republic* to drive two auto routes. We hauled newspapers to the young men who delivered them on bicycle. Our shifts began after midnight and lasted until 6 a.m.

Republic employees Bill Light and Dan Gerrard bundled our newspapers as they came off the press. We loaded them into our respective 1948 red Dodge pickups and headed across town. Dan eventually left the newspaper and became one of the Valley's most respected Episcopal priests. Rev. Dan Gerrard lived in Wickenburg, Arizona. He died in 2008.

After we delivered newspapers to the carriers, we delivered them to homes in more rural areas. After that, I would walk through the Papago Veterans Hospital, selling newspapers to patients. At 10 cents per newspaper sold and $1.25 per month per subscription, we made good money.

The first Sunday in January 1949 was a beautiful, sunny day. The upper McDowell and New River mountains were covered with new snow. The air was crisp.

After we were done delivering newspapers, Albert and I made plans for the rest of the day. We decided to pick up our girlfriends and drive north of Cave Creek, past Seven Springs, to see the snow.

I picked up Cora Ross and Albert brought Betty Westfall. We drove my pickup, which didn't have a heater. When we cleared the pass at Seven Springs, we saw more snow than we expected. From there, we decided to take Bloody Basin

Road, then head over to Black Canyon Road and drive home from there. We figured that we could turn around and go back the way we came if the road conditions deteriorated.

While traveling along Bloody Basin Road, we found an abandoned Cadillac. It was stuck crosswise, hubcap-deep in mud. A few yards away, there was another smaller road heading south. We took the bait, made the turn – and ended up stuck in the mud, too. Everyone bailed out and began pushing. I ended up spinning my truck's tires, covering my friends with water and mud. It was time for Plan B.

We decided to wait until dark after the ground froze. Then, we would shake the truck loose and drive out on the hard ground. Later that night, the mud did freeze. We got out of the truck and began rocking it back and forth, trying to break it free.

As it turned out, my truck had an "I" beam axle. Already immersed in mud, it was now frozen in it, too. Not only would the truck not budge, but we couldn't even shake it. The truck sat frozen in the mud. We sat in the cold truck. That night, the temperatures fell into the low teens. Our breath turned into icicles on the chrome parts of the truck's interior.

The next morning, Albert and I headed for Bumble Bee on foot, 15 miles away. As we hiked cross-country, a small airplane flew low overhead. The pilot dropped a 2-by-4 inch block of wood. It identified him as John Platt, a friend of our families.

He had volunteered to look for us. We motioned toward the truck where the girls were. He flew there and dropped another block of wood. Later that afternoon, a local rancher pulled the truck out of the mud, and we drove back to town late Monday night, getting home in time to go to work.

Meanwhile, word of our ordeal spread across town. *The Phoenix Gazette* carried a headline saying that we had been found. *The Arizona Republic* published a front-page story recounting our adventure.

That wasn't the only attention we received. When we completed our auto routes on Tuesday morning, we were welcomed back by Millan Leavett and Oliver King. They managed the newspaper's circulation department.

They told us that roughly 8,000 (out of a total of 75,000) copies of *The Arizona Republic* hadn't been dropped off to our auto route carriers on the morning of our absence, or had been misdelivered to carriers.

Although they didn't fire me or Albert, they offered us a decidedly different perspective on our adventure and its ramifications for customer service.

For my part, I eventually married Cora. We celebrated our 54th wedding anniversary in November 2004.

After completing their early morning newspaper routes the first Sunday in January 1949, Paul Messinger and his friend, Albert Owens, piled into Paul's 1948 red Dodge pickup truck with their girlfriends and headed for Bloody Basin Road. They unexpectedly got stuck in mud and snow and had to spend the night in the truck that had no heater. They got back to civilization the next day, with the help of a local rancher who pulled the truck out of the mud for them.

SCOTTSDALE HIGH WASN'T BIG, BUT IT HAD GREAT TEACHERS

Scottsdale Republic, April 1, 2005

We're often told that kids growing up in rural areas don't get the high-quality education available to students living in big cities. That may or may not be true. Part of the answer lies in defining a high-quality education.

For some, it's the size of the library or the newness of the buildings that counts. On those scores, big cities tend to score big. Nonetheless, I maintain that those of us who attended Scottsdale High School back in the 1940s weren't the least bit disadvantaged.

Back then, Scottsdale High had some great teachers. They knew their students well. For 60 years, from 1923 to 1983 (before it was eventually torn down), Scottsdale High educated generations of young people.

Since those days, I've had an opportunity to know, do business with or read about their accomplishments over these past many years. There were, of course, the famous ones – folks like Dan Quayle, who became vice-president, and Jim Palmer, the former major league pitcher. Other outstanding students included Russ Lyon, one of the Valley's major shopping center developers and Bill Schrader, former president of Salt River Project.

Scottsdale High also produced high-ranking military officers, as well as leaders of industry and all manner of professionals and teachers. These were solid family folk who became devoted parents.

Very special to me was a teacher named Leo J. Kennedy. He was my freshman science teacher back in 1944. There were 25 students in the class. To this day, six decades later, when I visit with those who took his courses, all of us remember how he opened up a whole world of fact and scientific logic. My appetite for engineering was fostered in his class. I still remember his laboratory demonstrations.

Because Scottsdale High was so small, we all knew Leo, his family and where they lived. He knew as much about each of us. We saw him as a teacher and a family man. He moved to Escondido, California, my sophomore year. My family and others kept in touch with him for years.

Others who taught mathematics and science included Mr. Allen, Mr. W.P. Healy, Mr. Polster, Ms. Seitz and Mr. Waldorf, as well as William Whatcott and Cecil McGirr (who taught two generations of Messingers).

These teachers often researched subjects of special interest to individual students. For example, Mr. Whatcott taught me and my friend, Albert Owens, solid geometry and spherical trigonometry. He sat in a student desk while we did our work on the blackboard.

Many teachers, like Mr. Whatcott, took on extra teaching hours to help aspiring students. In some cases, the teachers were learning right along with us. It created a positive educational atmosphere.

Other teachers who paid a lot of individual attention to me and my classmates included Maybelle Olson, Leldon C. Windes, Mary Jane Belluzzi, Leslie Fairbanks, Margaret Means, William P. "Dub" Davis, Bill Manes, Earl Jones and Herman Schweikart.

Scottsdale High wasn't big by "big city" standards. We didn't have a lot of the things kids take for granted today. But what we did have were devoted teachers and a learning environment second to none.

A lot of well-known people graduated from the old Scottsdale High School that used to be located on the north side of Indian School Road, east of Scottsdale Road. Some of the school's more notable graduates included former Vice President Dan Quayle; Jim Palmer, the former major league pitcher; Russ Lyon, one of the Valley's major developers; and Bill Schrader, former president of Salt River Project.

HIGH SCHOOL TENNIS WAS A DIFFERENT GAME DURING '40s

Scottsdale Republic, April 15, 2005

Back in the 1940s, tiny Scottsdale High School played tennis against the big schools. We challenged giants like Phoenix Union, the Mesa Jackrabbits and various Tucson schools at state tennis tournaments. Both the boys' and girls' teams were successful in those days.

Leldon C. Windes, Scottsdale High's tennis coach, had been a former Border Conference champion at Arizona State College (now Arizona State University) a few years earlier. If he hadn't contracted polio, he might have become a professional tennis player.

Instead, he became a teacher. He spent his entire career at Scottsdale High teaching history, typing and business. He also oversaw the students who put out the yearbook and coached tennis.

Windes was a member of one of Arizona's oldest families, pioneers who came to live in the Verde Valley before the advent of the Civil War. As such, he loved history and did a good deal of research on Scottsdale pioneer Winfield Scott (after whom Scottsdale would one day be named).

In 1943, Coach Windes' high school tennis stars included folks like Gerry Thompson, John Sander, Allen Abney, Mavis Carroll and Bernice Sharp. They were followed by Dick Davidson, Bill Schrader, Bonnie Treat, Francis Sharp, Joan Walt and Lorraine Cooper.

By 1948, the men's team featured Albert Owens, David Goodburn, Wally Platt, John Mayo and myself.

The women players included Betty Westfall, Cora Ross, Jeanette Owens, Virginia Holly and Jo Ann Schmuck.

Back then, high school tennis was played differently than it is today. Boys didn't wear shorts and the surface of the court was concrete. If a ball hit a crack and bounced sideways, that's just the way it was. There usually was dirt on the court, too, so tennis shoes didn't grip very well.

I wore long pants and cowboy boots when I played tennis. That way, I could run and then slide when going after the ball.

The tennis rackets were made of wood and strung with cat gut. The great tennis names of the time (people like Don Budge and Wilmer Hines) were printed on the rackets. Sixty-plus years later, it's doubtful that many of today's young players have ever heard of them.

Windes owned a 1941 four-door Plymouth. If he had to teach a class at the same time that the girls' team had a tennis match, he just gave one of the girls his keys. The whole team piled into the car and off they went. Imagine a coach doing that today.

In 1948, Cora Ross (whom I married in 1950) and Jo Ann Schmuck represented Scottsdale High at the state finals. They played in the doubles competition. Unfortunately, they were beaten in the third set and didn't win the title.

Cora continued to play tennis for pleasure, giving up the game in the mid-1990s. Her tennis days at Scottsdale High led to more than 50 years of great exercise and rewarded her with many close friends.

Leland C. Windes taught history, typing and business at Scottsdale High School. He also coached both the boys' and girls' tennis teams. Both Paul and Cora Messinger played under Coach Windes. Paul recalls that he wore jeans and cowboy boots when he played tennis, so he could run and then slide when going after the ball. Pictured here are the girls of the 1949 tennis team.

A PRIME OPPORTUNITY MISSED: NE VALLEY LAND FOR $10 AN ACRE

Scottsdale Republic, April 29, 2005

In the 1940s, when Scottsdale real estate salesmen couldn't find a tourist or a newcomer in town, they would stop by *The Arizona Republic/The Phoenix Gazette* newspaper stations to see if any of the paperboys wanted to buy some land.

This happened several times while I was a newspaper carrier. One incident in particular stands out in my mind.

A fellow by the name of John Utter, of Utter Realty, came by one day and offered to sell land to Billie Wilson, Willie Duncan and myself, among others. It came in 10-acre parcels on the edge of Paradise Valley (north of today's Central Arizona Project canal, stretching to Dynamite Road).

He was asking $10 an acre. With interest, deed and other costs factored into the deal, the price came to $10 a month for a year. In other words, I could have purchased 10 acres of vacant desert land for $120.

When I asked my dad (who was both a lawyer and a rancher) about buying the 10 acres, he said the land had no water and that its true value was closer to 50 cents, or maybe $1, per acre. Furthermore, he said it would take half a section (several hundred acres) to support one or two cows.

I thought about what my dad said and decided not to buy the land.

Wilson made a different decision and purchased a single 10-acre site. I've often wondered how long he kept the land and what kind of return he got on his $120 investment.

Then again, maybe I don't want to know.

A few years later (by the early to mid-1950s), land in what today is north Scottsdale was selling for $350 per acre. Those same 10-acre parcels for $120 were now going for $3,500. A lot of folks who were new to town bought them up.

In contrast, we longtime locals were "too smart" to buy that worthless land. Besides, we didn't have any money to invest even if we had wanted to. We were too busy building new homes and churches, and taxing ourselves to construct new schools, roads and the other infrastructure that was needed to sustain the area's rapid growth.

About a decade later, in the early 1960s, my wife, Cora, and I were in the early years of building our funeral business. We wanted to build a cemetery to complement our mortuary and needed a lot of land. Once again, all eyes turned north where vacant desert land extended for miles.

We also turned to Guy Stillman (whose family owned McCormick Ranch). Scottsdale recently had annexed land north of Shea Boulevard and Stillman had obtained a cemetery use permit for one of those parcels.

In 1966, we purchased some of Stillman's land, about one-half mile east of Pima Road, for $1,875 per acre. It seemed very expensive at the time.

Over time, Cora, myself and Stillman brought A.L. Moore, Chester Hansen, Larry J. Melcher, Ralph Sage and Paul Beer into the partnership.

They helped cover the cost of the land, as well as the cost of turning it into a cemetery. It was a big project – and a successful one. In 1983, we were able to buy out our partners.

By 1989, Cora and I had spent 31 years covering the nighttime telephones for our mortuary. After three decades, it was time to leave that duty to others. So, I purchased an acre of land just north of our cemetery site. That's where we decided to build our current home. That one acre of empty desert cost us $79,500!

How I wish that I had bought those 10 acres for $10 apiece some 40 years earlier. It was the same dirt then as it is today.

What did we learn from this experience? The value of a piece of land isn't tied to the number of cows it can support.

In 1966, Paul and Cora Messinger bought land from Guy Stillman (whose family also owned McCormick Ranch) to build a cemetery north of Shea Blvd., about a half mile east of Pima Road. Over time, A.L. Moore, Chester Hansen, Larry J. Melcher, Ralph Sage and Paul Beer (all local mortuary owners) bought into the cemetery. In 1983, the Messingers bought out their partners and Paradise Memorial Gardens eventually expanded to also include a mausoleum and crematory.

CARNIVAL GAVE SCOTTSDALE RESIDENTS SOMETHING FUN TO DO

Scottsdale Republic, May 27, 2005

At least once a year, the carnival traveled across the empty desert to Scottsdale.

It consisted of a Ferris wheel, a merry-go-round, a Loop-O-Plane, several games of chance and all kinds of fun foods. There was plenty of entertainment for us kids and young people. The carnival atmosphere even energized the older folks.

When it arrived, it took a day, sometimes two, to unload the big trucks and put the rides and midway booths together. The carnival managers sometimes would hire local teenagers to help. They would carry the many pieces of the rides and booths to the places where they finally would be assembled.

I tried to get one of those jobs a couple of times, but my friends would get there first and land them. All I could do was stand around and watch, hopeful that I could claim some special expertise and a job the following year when the good times would return.

The carnival used to set up on a piece of vacant land west of the old Red Brick School House, south of where the *Yearlings* statue stands near Main Street and Brown Avenue.

This annual event usually came to town during the summer months, but the heat never kept anyone away. Besides, other than the local pool hall (which was a lot of fun), there wasn't much else to do.

Scottsdale back then didn't have a movie theater, a bowling alley, a skating rink, a public swimming pool or any other form of organized entertainment. These, and other amenities, weren't built until the late 1940s and early 1950s.

If you wanted to be entertained, you had to leave town. Phoenix held a rodeo once a year. It also had a movie theater. And Tempe operated a swimming pool at Tempe Beach Park. That's why, for Scottsdale kids, the carnival was such a big deal. We looked forward to its arrival.

One evening I was standing where Saba's Western Store sits today, along with Oscar Strobel, a nationally known local artist, and my friend, Willie Duncan. We wondered aloud whether it would be more interesting to watch the folks enjoy the carnival or go enjoy the rides and games ourselves. It was a tough choice. After all, people-watching can be pretty entertaining.

For example, when families arrived, the adults would pass out handfuls of dimes and quarters to the children. Within minutes, with hands outstretched, the little ones would be back for more.

Moms and dads would try to slow the flow of money from their purses and wallets while impatient youths did their best to keep those dimes and quarters coming. We stood there listening to their enthusiastic pleas. It didn't take long for the eagerness of youth to melt their parents' hearts – and then their pocketbooks.

As I think back on Scottsdale's traveling carnival, I remember the feelings of anticipation when it arrived and the excitement of watching it rise, piece by piece, out of the ground. I'm also reminded of the special smells and all of the funny sounds that the carnival brought to our small, rural town.

All of us had to work during the hot summer months, often outdoors. We picked watermelons, made hay, mowed lawns and did all sorts of odd jobs. As hard as the work might have been, we had a good time. But, at our ages, it was the wonderful summer evenings at the carnival that made our young lives so worth living.

At least once a year, the carnival traveled across the empty desert and set up on a piece of vacant land west of the old Red Brick School House, south of where the Yearlings statue stands near Main Street and Brown Avenue. It consisted of a Ferris wheel, a merry-go-round, a Loop-O-Plane, several games of chance and all kinds of fun foods.

YOUNG MAN'S LESSON IN FAIR TREATMENT NEVER FORGOTTEN

Scottsdale Republic, June 10, 2005

In the 1950s, we always irrigated the yard surrounding our first home. It was on the south side of Indian School Road, just east of Miller Road.

Generally speaking, a day or so after I ordered the water that we needed, we were given an assigned time to open our irrigation valve and flood our lawn. More often than not, our irrigation water was scheduled to arrive during the early morning hours. Times like 2:00 a.m. and 3:30 a.m. weren't uncommon.

We were a small water user compared with the big farms. Back then, farmers received 30 or more hours of water at a time. We were given our water in between these large users.

One evening, in the summer of 1959, I forgot that I was scheduled to receive my irrigation water later that night. I slept right through it.

The next morning, shortly after I got to my office, my neighbor, Art Zeleny, came by. He said his house had been flooded earlier that morning. As soon as he told me what had happened, I remembered that I hadn't irrigated like I was supposed to.

I immediately confessed.

Zeleny's house was on Second Street, one block east of Miller Road. It was the old farmhouse that sat on a 40-acre site that eventually became a subdivision called Peaceful Valley. Zeleny operated a small meat-cutting business on the property that served farmers and hunters in the Scottsdale area.

His story went like this: His wife, Geraldine, had gotten up early that morning and stepped out of bed into 3 inches of water that was streaming through their bedroom. In essence, my unused share of the irrigation water had backed up in the Zeleny home.

Geraldine and their daughter, Patricia, were amateur artists. There they were, in the wee hours of the morning, lifting their paintings out of the water, along with all sorts of books and other items that were sitting on the floor.

Meanwhile, Art shoveled sand around their front door to block more water from coming in. Then they began mopping up.

Their carpets and throw rugs were soaked. They pulled them up and squeezed out what water they could before taking them to Phoenix for cleaning. After they were finished wiping off the floors and bottoms of the walls, they opened the doors and windows and dried out their home.

That's when Art came over to see me. He wasn't mad. In fact, he was really quite patient as he stood there telling me what had happened. I felt terrible and assured him that I would take responsibility, and I called my insurance carrier after he left.

Later that day, an agent called me back and told me that my policy didn't cover failures to act that resulted in damage to someone else's property. However, since we were a new account, he offered to send out an adjuster to help determine the value of the loss so I could settle with Art. I was told that I would have to pay whatever losses we mutually agreed to.

Art felt $125 (the cost of getting his carpets cleaned) would be a reasonable settlement. His even-handed approach so impressed the seasoned insurance adjuster that he recommended the company pay the $125. And that's what it did.

My wife, Cora, and I were in our 20s and in our first year in business when the Zeleny flood occurred. To this day, when we negotiate with others, we remember how fairly Art treated us. We try to figure out what our true losses or costs are, and then do what's right.

We were so blessed to be given this lesson at such a formative time in our lives.
I hope others find value in this story.

In the 1950s, Scottsdale residents kept their grass green and their trees alive using flood irrigation. One night, Paul Messinger forgot to get up during the night to open his irrigation valve. This caused his neighbor's house to flood throughout with at least three inches of water. Paul confessed to his error and offered to pay for the damages. To this day, Paul remembers how patient and kind his neighbor was in light of Paul's negligence.

TOLERANCE ALLOWS US TO ENJOY RICH, DIVERSE, EDUCATIONAL FRIENDSHIPS

Scottsdale Republic, July 22, 2005

My wife, Cora, and I recently joined our longtime friends, Bob and Audree Beal, for a special Sunday breakfast. They were celebrating a wedding anniversary.

During our conversation, the subject of political tolerance came up. Audree pointed out how folks can hold differing views on a whole range of subjects and still remain friends.

Her comment made me think back to the special legislative election that was held in 1979. I ran against my good friend, Bill Jenkins, for the vacant seat after the death of State Senator David Kret. His district encompassed most of Scottsdale.

When it became apparent we would be running against one another, Bill and I agreed that two weeks after the elections were over, the winner would buy the other guy and his wife the best steak in town.

Two weeks after the election, Cora and I shared an excellent meal at the Camelback Inn with Bill and Sue Jenkins. Bill and I remained lifelong friends. He died in 2008.

We're fortunate to live in a country where folks can be poles apart politically and still remain friends. In this same regard, another friend recently opined, "In America, we don't hate people of different political philosophies."

His declaration caused me to reflect on the many people, here in Scottsdale and elsewhere, that Cora and I consider our friends. They include Democrats, Republicans, Libertarians, Independents and all shades of political beliefs in between.

Over these many years, we've been strong proponents of our ideas while respecting those who have differing points of view. Just because we might disagree with a particular person's political philosophy doesn't mean we can't call him or her "friend."

That said, I must admit that it's sometimes easier to have friends who share beliefs similar to my own. Still, that's not a requirement for friendship. Some of my more "far out" friends often pose challenging questions. They take stands that cause me to evaluate my own way of thinking.

Throughout my life, people with views contrary to my own helped me formulate my own political philosophy. Openly sharing differing points of view with friends is a healthy thing to do. It's what many hope the people of Iraq will begin to master.

Like my friend Audree, I hope those who read this column also appreciate the importance of tolerance and the wide range of ideas and friendships that it can foster over one's lifetime. This includes tolerance for religious faiths, national origin, race and so many other, and often minor, differences between people.

It's more than a way of thinking. It's a blessing for us all.

Bill and Sue Jenkins (pictured) and Paul and Cora Messinger remained lifelong friends, despite the fact that Paul and Bill ran against each other in a special legislative election in 1979.

CAMELBACK CEMETERY HOLDS MANY PIONEERS

Scottsdale Republic, August 19, 2005

Many people who drive past the little desert cemetery on McDonald Drive one-half mile west of Scottsdale Road wonder how it came to be.

They also wonder who's buried there.

It's a humble place, but its grounds are well-kept and dotted with special grave markers.

In the early 1900s, Hans and Mary Weaver homesteaded 160 acres on what now is East McDonald Drive. In 1915, their daughter, Hattie, married Adolph Frank Poenicke.

Three weeks after the wedding, he fell ill and died. The Weavers decided to bury him on their land, which was a fairly common practice in those times. A year later, they decided to dedicate two acres of their land, which included their son-in-law's grave, as a community cemetery.

They prepared a simple, hand-written dedication and named it Camelback Cemetery, after the familiar mountain one mile to the west. The documents identified the locations of each grave and a small network of streets and paths.

The signed dedication was published and recorded, and the cemetery became the first to serve greater Scottsdale. The land was formally donated by the Weavers to a governing body called the Camelback Cemetery Association. Over the years, many locals have served on its board. Jean Scott, who died in June 2005, had volunteered for more than 30 years.

A year after the Weavers dedicated the cemetery, Mary died. Born in 1857, she was buried there in 1917. Hans died some years later and is buried next to her.

Hattie married Thomas Coldwell. They had two children and two stepchildren. After Thomas' death, Hattie married Roy Peterson. She died in 1962 and is buried at Double Butte Cemetery in Tempe.

Until the end of World War II, most graves were dug with a pick and a shovel. Gravediggers used to pour a milk can's worth of water on the ground, wait a few hours for it to sink in, and then dig. They would repeat the process over and over again.

As such, it often took the better part of two days to dig a standard 6-foot grave. Today, that same grave is dug with a backhoe in a couple of hours.

The cemetery has 992 grave sites and has been in continuous use since its founding. Many of Scottsdale's pioneer families and prominent citizens are buried there.

We have been opening and closing graves at this same 90-year old cemetery for 47 years. Interestingly, some people have taken it upon themselves to hand-dig graves for their family members and friends. Occasionally, we'll lend assistance to those who try. I have great respect for those who finally succeed.

Camelback Cemetery on McDonald Drive one-half mile west of Scottsdale Road became a cemetery in 1916. The cemetery has 992 grave sites and has been in continuous use since its founding. Many of Scottsdale's pioneer families and prominent citizens are buried here.

CHOIR PRACTICE TAUGHT WHEN TO SING LOUDLY, WHEN TO SPEAK SOFTLY

Scottsdale Republic, September 16, 2005

When my family arrived in Arizona, before we moved to what then was the little farming community of Scottsdale, we settled in Phoenix.

Once we were established, my mother believed that my siblings and I should continue our religious education in our new hometown.

The First Congregational Church of Phoenix became our church. It was the only congregational church in Phoenix in the 1940s. We had been members of the Park Congregational Church in Grand Rapids, Michigan, before moving to Phoenix, so it made sense to join the congregational church here.

Several months later, my folks purchased a 20-acre farm on the southeastern corner of Miller and Indian School Roads in Scottsdale. We were so busy that first winter after our move that we attended our Phoenix church only a few times.

By summer, my mom was worried about our religious education once again. This time, she sent my brother, Phil, to the First Baptist Church's summer school, which was down the street at Brown and Indian School Roads (where Chase Bank's drive-through windows are today).

It was on a Friday during the second week of summer school when my mom, while hanging up the family laundry in the backyard, spotted a dozen or so students – including Phil, along with the church minister and a teacher – walking east on Indian School Road. She greeted them as they walked by.

At the time, my mom assumed that they were on some kind of a field trip. But about 30 minutes later, when the group passed by again, heading west and dripping wet, she realized the purpose of their trip – they had walked to nearby Schrader's Pond to be baptized. Phil, who had been baptized as a baby with a sprinkling of water, now as a young man, was just baptized by immersion.

My mom and our family were comfortable with Phil's second baptism. After all, it was far better to have been baptized twice than not at all.

A few years later, when I was a teenager, I attended the local Methodist church. It was there that I joined the Methodist Youth Fellowship, also known as the MYF. Mrs. Vera Pasley was my teacher.

One spring, the church decided to organize a teenage choir. It was supposed to relieve the adult choir during the summer months. All of the "MYFers" (including myself) were tasked with practicing to become that backup choir. We practiced every Wednesday for many weeks.

The first Sunday in June finally arrived. We took our place in the choir section in the front of the church and enthusiastically sang each of the songs planned for that day's service.

Much to our surprise, though, we were told at choir practice the following Wednesday that we wouldn't be needed anymore that summer. I thought we had sounded pretty good. Since then, I've been told that I'm somewhat tone-deaf.

Looking back, it's pretty obvious to me that only a small percentage of the folks in any church are really capable of singing. Accordingly, I've learned over these 60-plus years that when in church, it's best to quietly speak the words of the hymns and not try to take the lead.

This is the only known picture of Scottsdale Methodist Church in its original form. The image is taken from a very rare ceramic tile on which the image was etched by an artist. The tile is owned by Helen Hughes.

SCOTTSDALE METHODIST CHURCH
Scottsdale, Arizona
1929 - 1956

CEMETERY FIREHOUSE AN EXAMPLE OF PIONEERING SPIRIT

Scottsdale Republic, September 30, 2005

In the early 1970s, when Paradise Memorial Gardens cemetery opened, the 9300 block of East Shea Boulevard was paved two lanes wide. Few homes were built that far north and east at the time.

Still, the need for police and fire protection was becoming more of a concern. The closest fire service came from stations far to the west, and the police station was in downtown Scottsdale, not too far from where the main police headquarters are today.

Desert Springs Water Co. provided domestic water, but there were few or no fire hydrants. Another company, Rural/Metro Fire Department, had a contract with the city to provide firefighting services.

To fight fires, Rural/Metro had to carry water on its trucks or pump water from nearby swimming pools or cattle tanks. It learned how to operate with limited water supplies and actually kept the area's annual fire losses far below the national average.

Like everyone else out our way, we had no fire hydrant to protect our buildings – in this case, our cemetery offices. I called Lou Witzeman, the founder and owner of Rural/Metro, and asked him for advice on how we could protect ourselves against a possible fire.

He noted that we had a one-acre lake on our property and he suggested that we install a "dry" fire hydrant. He had seen one on a trip to Europe. It's called "dry" because, unlike a normal fire hydrant, it's not connected to a pressurized source of water.

Instead, we had to prime our "dry" hydrant with a couple of hundred gallons of water. That allowed us to pump water from our lake through a pipe connecting the hydrant to the lake. More than thirty years later, we still have that "dry" hydrant.

A few years after we installed the "dry" hydrant, Witzeman came to see me. He was looking for a place to locate a fire station to serve areas along Shea Boulevard, east of 90th Street. He wanted to lease some land and build a fire station.

I suggested that he add a firetruck garage to the side of an office building that we weren't using. We could turn the office into a dormitory, complete with a full bath. The telephones were already installed.

Witzeman explained that the city planned to build a permanent fire station farther east. In the meantime, though, he took me up on my offer, and we built a temporary fire station at the cemetery that provided fire protection for northeast Scottsdale for 18 months.

Every once in awhile, I run into an old firefighter who worked out of the cemetery station. Those moments remind me of the pioneering spirit exemplified by Witzeman and the staff of Rural/Metro. We all worked together to provide a vital service to a community beset by growing pains.

Lou Witzeman was the founder of Rural/Metro Fire Department, which provided fire and ambulance services to Scottsdale for decades before the city established its own municipal fire department. At one time, Rural/Metro ran a temporary fire station for 18 months out of Messinger's Paradise Memorial Gardens cemetery at Shea Blvd. and 92nd Street.

SCOTTSDALE HIGH WAS A POWERHOUSE IN 6-MAN FOOTBALL

Scottsdale Republic, October 14, 2005

When Scottsdale High School was our only high school, and it had fewer than 100 students, we played what was known as six-man football. It made for a great game that was exciting to watch.

The scores were more like those you would expect to see in basketball. Why? Because in six-man football, everyone except the center was an eligible pass receiver.

Since so many players on each team could catch the ball, every defensive player had to play man-on-man to effectively cover the pass.

Likewise, the defensive center had to play opposite the offensive center to prevent a running play. To make the defense even more difficult, teams often used spread formations. Each team had three downs to make 15 yards.

One time we beat a team called Fort Thomas 99-0. They didn't have much of a quarterback, and we ran up the score (something that we shouldn't have done). In some respects, six-man football was like watching Arizona State University, back in the fabled Frank Kush days.

In addition to Fort Thomas, we played teams like the Litchfield Owls, Gilbert Tigers and Peoria Panthers. The rivalry among these six-man teams was just as fierce as any conference composed of 11-man teams, then or today. Maybe even more so.

When we played Wickenburg, we played in the bottom of the Hassayampa River. Wickenburg's players used to come out of their three-point stance with handfuls of sand they would pitch into the faces of the opposition at the beginning of a play.

It's tough to catch a pass, or make a defensive play, with dirt in your eyes. While there were local rules against the practice, they didn't prevent infractions.

Few playing fields of that era were as good as the fields of today. And, for its day, Wickenburg's field was the worst!

Some of the Scottsdale High football coaches who led us to victory in the 1940s included Bill Manes, William P. "Dub" Davis and Richard B. "Jiggs" Hardt. The latter two are in the Scottsdale Quarterback Club's Hall of Fame.

Star players at the time included Junior Howard, Bob Spradling, Joe Pastorino, Londo Pastorino, Bob Zimmerman, Red Perry, Carl Cluff and Russ Lyon. They weren't the best-trained athletes, but these and other young men around town were solid farm folk. They were physically fit and very resourceful.

We always had the feeling that we were winners. And, indeed, we often were. Scottsdale High's six-man football teams were conference champions several times during the 1940s.

During those years, Scottsdale High also fielded fine basketball and baseball teams, as well as boys' and girls' tennis teams. They enjoyed enthusiastic community support, partly because there were few forms of entertainment available and because our teams were consistently successful.

1947 CONFERENCE GAMES		
Scottsdale Beavers	Opponents	
41	Ft. Thomas	27
46	Hayden	30
55	Litchfield	14
43	Wickenburg	28
27	Peoria	2
12	Gilbert	14
45	Tolleson	7
49	Litchfield	26
47	Wickenburg	8
57	Peoria	13
22	Gilbert	19
11 games — 444		188
Avg. game score: 40.36		17.09

Scottsdale High School's six-man football teams were conference champions several times during the 1940s, including this 10-1 season in 1947

BODY SHOP ONCE BAILED YOUNG MOTORIST OUT OF TROUBLE

Scottsdale Republic, October 28, 2005

Do you remember the "Basket House" on Brown Avenue in downtown Scottsdale? It was an interesting place, containing every kind of basket that you could imagine.

Sax Pettit and his wife, Ercell, traveled the world looking for unique baskets to import. You could take a trip around the world without leaving their store. Today, the current owners feature Western culture and art.

The store started out as Tamm's Market in the 1920s. Later, it became A.E. Mahoney's Market and still later Davis' Market. In the early 1940s, a man named Zeph opened a body and fender shop on the site. He lived in the back of the building.

When Zeph left, the building became a local Assembly of God Church. Years later, the congregation built a new church. That's when Sax and Ercell opened the Basket House, much loved by locals and visitors alike.

My memories of the place are important to me. As such, it is with great sentimentality that I recall one evening in 1947 when Zeph's body and fender shop was located there.

I was driving my dad's 1937 International pickup. I was following my friend Albert Owens. Being a young driver, I was following too closely. When Albert suddenly stopped, my truck rear-ended his dad's 1941 International pickup!

In those days, pickups came from the factory without rear bumpers. Folks in this part of the country generally went to the local blacksmith to have solid iron bumpers and trailer hitches installed.

Albert's pickup was no exception. When the pickup I was driving hit the one he was driving, the front bumper on my pickup went underneath the back end bumper on his pickup. The crash wiped out my headlights, the grille and the radiator and also dented the pickup's heavy-gauge front fenders. Albert's pickup was undamaged.

Knowing what my dad would say, I immediately went over and asked Zeph if he would open up his garage and assess the damage, which was pretty severe. I asked him if he could fix the truck that night (which really seemed impossible).

He was a nice man and sympathetic to my plight. He had a great suggestion. He said that he knew of a man on the Salt River Indian Reservation who had the same model pickup that I had. It had been hit in the rear and wrecked and was sitting in the man's yard.

Zeph suggested I go see him and buy the headlights, grille, radiator and radiator frame off his pickup. Prices were a lot less then, and Zeph suggested offering him $25 or $30, which he felt was fair.

We drove over to the man's house, made the deal and removed the parts with some tools Zeph loaned to us. Meanwhile, back at his shop, Zeph stripped the front off of my dad's pickup and began straightening the dented fenders.

By midnight we had the truck reassembled. Zeph thought the job would look a lot better if we painted the truck. We masked off the parts that didn't need painting and Zeph painted the pickup its original color, International green.

When I got home the next morning at 4:30 a.m. (in time to milk the cows on our dairy farm), I showed my dad how nice his truck looked with its new paint job. I explained that we had "slightly" bumped it, so it only seemed right to fix it and the new coat of paint was a nice touch. Later, my dad heard the small-town rumors that gave him a more detailed report of the accident.

We had that truck for many years thereafter. In fact, I grew skilled enough at auto mechanics that I overhauled the engine. My friends and I ended up rebuilding several old cars. Some were substantially modified and became the local Scottsdale "hot rods" of their day.

A man named "Zeph" operated a body and fender shop on Brown Avenue in downtown Scottsdale in the 1940s. One night in 1947, Zeph kindly helped a young Paul Messinger repair damages Paul had inflicted on his dad's 1937 International pickup. It took all night, but Paul returned the truck to his dad at 4:30 the next morning when he showed up for his morning milking chores on the family dairy.

BUSING TO ASU FOOTBALL WAS SOCIAL EVENT FOR SCOTTSDALE

Scottsdale Republic, November 11, 2005

When I think back to those Arizona State University football games of the 1950s, '60s and '70s, and legendary Sun Devils coach Frank Kush, I remember that the games were always played on Saturday nights.

Each was the social event of the week, a bigger event then than now.

The social aspects of college football were appealing. The games always started at 8:00 p.m. My wife, Cora, and I and our Scottsdale friends would meet at Scottsdale restaurants before the games. The restaurants would arrange, for a nominal fee, for buses to take us to Sun Devil Stadium and bring us back.

This gave us plenty of time to eat and talk before boarding the buses for Tempe. The university provided an area northeast of the stadium entrance for buses to unload and then park during the game.

Back then, games didn't last as long as they do today because so few of them were televised. There were no breaks in the action to accommodate commercials. No time was spent "reviewing" tapes of officiating calls.

A large percentage of the folks who traveled to the stadium arrived and left by bus. That meant most of the spectators stayed in their seats until the game was over. The buses weren't going anywhere until it ended, and everyone who came on the bus got back on the bus.

Frank Kush football was a special kind of football. For some reason, his teams often were considered the underdog, even though they won more than 75 percent of their games. Kush teams were fast, and they played as a team.

For his part, Kush was a great motivator and teacher. He wanted his teams to be in better physical condition than their opponents. His teams were extremely disciplined.

The young men on those teams gave Kush and his coaching staff their all. We saw game after game, some of the finest college football in America in those days. Many talented players made it in professional football after playing for Kush.

When the buses returned us to Scottsdale, folks usually drove over to the old Safari Hotel to grab a bite at Paul Shank's Coffee House. Everyone was hungry and excited about having seen a great game. We were looking for a place to share our thoughts about the action.

It became a routine for so many people that you often had to stand in line 30 minutes to an hour to get inside if your bus got back late.

Paul Shank's Coffee House was large and the service was fast. But the crowds were larger. I don't know of any other restaurants, then or now, where customers would wait in line from 11:30 p.m. to 1:00 a.m.

Today, Shank's restaurants (his coffee shop, The French Quarter and Paul Shank's Gracious Dining) are gone, along with the elegant Safari Hotel. The giant fleets of buses are gone, too.

ASU football rarely is as exciting as it was back then. Regardless, those of us who supported those teams from the '50s through the '70s still attend. We're getting older, but we still love to watch the Sun Devils win.

Times have changed. Now, we have to drive ourselves to the daytime games, which are controlled by television networks, and eat alone or purchase fast food from a stadium concessionaire.

Nonetheless, we love ASU football. We're thankful for the good times in the past – and still long for more of what we so enjoyed way back when.

During the halcyon days of Coach Frank Kush's tenure at Arizona State University, going to the Saturday football game was the social event of the week. Locals would meet friends at Scottsdale restaurants, where fans could enjoy good food and leisurely visits before boarding buses that took them to Sun Devil Stadium in Tempe for the 8 p.m. kick-off.

© *Scottsdale Republic*, Nov. 11, 2005, photograph by Rob Schumacher. Used with permission. Permission does not imply endorsement.

RAISING TURKEYS YIELDS TONS OF MEMORIES

Scottsdale Republic, November 25, 2005

The nation was at war in the 1940s. Travel was limited. Still, families that lived in Scottsdale and around the Northeast Valley came together for Thanksgiving much as we do today.

But those who lived farther away couldn't join us. Air travel was in its infancy, even in the late 1940s. Back then, few people flew or had ever flown.

For our family, Thanksgiving also meant that we had to help my mom with her big cash crop: her flock of plump turkeys! Thanksgiving week was the culmination of much of her year's worth of work. She started raising turkeys in early spring of 1943, when she purchased two broad-breasted bronze hens and a tom.

From those first two hens – including one that she named "Eleanor" – she produced 40 offspring. She sold 30 turkeys that first Thanksgiving and held back 10 birds so she could grow a larger flock the following year. Her plan worked. By Thanksgiving 1944, my mom took 250 turkeys to market.

Do you know how long it takes to catch a turkey selected on sight by a customer? Then, you had to hang it on the clothesline and kill it with an instant cut to the spinal cord and jugular vein.

The next step involved quickly picking off the big feathers and singeing off the "pin" feathers over a small gas stove in the barn. Finally, we had to remove the innards, remove the lower legs and head, weigh the bird and wrap it. We charged 35 cents per pound.

We followed this same routine more than 200 times in 1944. Mom grossed more than $1,200 during those Thanksgiving weeks. That was a lot of money back then. As such, her business was quite profitable. Except for a little starter mash for the chicks and some rolled barley to keep the turkeys coming home at night, the only other expense was the grain needed to finally fatten the birds.

The turkeys were free to "range" much of their lives, living off the land on and around my dad's dairy farm. I don't think we ever spent more than $300 on feed in any given year. Sometimes we spent a lot less – as little as $175 during the summer and fall.

No matter how many birds my mom raised, we rarely had enough for everyone who wanted one. Sometimes, she would sell one of her brood hens if a customer seemed disappointed about not getting a turkey.

When Thanksgiving turkey sales were over, it was our turn to enjoy our own Thanksgiving feast. In those days, turkeys didn't have to be defrosted because frozen turkeys were pretty much unknown. In our case, we just went out back and plucked one.

My family celebrated Thanksgiving in all sorts of different places. One year it might be in our backyard. Another year, it might be in Papago Park or at Black Mountain near the Verde River.

I don't ever remember it raining on Thanksgiving. Then again, maybe I'm only remembering the good times. Of course, rain or shine, sharing Thanksgiving Day with family and friends always was a good time.

A lot of important events in my life coincide with Thanksgiving Day. I married Cora on Thanksgiving. And, one year, my dad, my brother and I decided to start Messinger Mortuary after a delicious Thanksgiving meal.

Every now and then, depending upon the year, my birthday falls on Thanksgiving Day. We often had pecan pie on those occasions because it's always been my favorite.

One of the Messinger boys' chores every November was the catching, slaughtering and removal of feathers from the turkeys their mom raised on the family farm. In 1944, the boys rounded up and prepared more than 200 turkeys for customers. They charged 35 cents per pound for the birds, and Vera Messinger grossed $1,200 in 1944 from her birds.

BUILDING BROODER HOUSE REVEALED JOYS OF CONSTRUCTION

Scottsdale Republic, January 6, 2006

Over the Christmas break from school back in 1942, my parents had just begun farming the 20 acres that they owned on the southeastern corner of Miller and Indian School Roads, a stone's throw from downtown Scottsdale.

They had purchased the land with the intent of turning it into a working dairy and poultry farm.

One of the first things we needed was a brooder house, a building that could shelter up to 500 baby chicks. With the approach of spring, we needed the brooder house right away if we were going to raise laying hens old enough to produce eggs by summer. Later on, we built hen houses, a milking barn, a feed house and a shop area.

Jack and Lillian Stewart were our neighbors. They lived across the street, north of Indian School Road. Although they were well along in years, they were active professionals. They knew farming and ranching. As such, it came as no surprise when Jack offered to help build our first brooder house.

We began by drawing a simple plan for a building measuring 12 feet wide by 12 feet long. It had a pitched gable roof, a door facing east, and two sets of lift-up plastic windows looking south. We built the house on 3-by-12-inch wooden skids. That way, if the building ended up in the wrong place, we could use our tractor to pull it where it needed to go. Needless to say, all of this construction occurred before the city required building permits.

My dad purchased the necessary building supplies at the Hayes Lumber Yard. It stood on the east side of Scottsdale Road, where the Pink Pony restaurant operated for many years.

Stewart didn't use power tools. We didn't either. So, we sawed all of the wooden planks by hand.

First, we put down the flat runners, as well as the bracing that held them together. Then, we nailed down the tongue-and-groove pine floor. Next, we framed the 2-by-4 walls and stood them up. The roof rafters and sheeting were nailed to the walls, and wooden shingles made up the finished roof. Lastly, we covered the outside of the exposed stud wall with wooden siding. Except for painting, we finished the brooder house in a single day.

Building our family's first brooder house was my first real construction experience. It was so much fun that a week later my dad decided it might be wise to have two brooder houses. We built the second house just like the first one, and when we were done, we strung an electric line from our home to both buildings.

In late January 1943, we received 500 day-old leghorn chicks from a fellow named George Haws, who lived in Lehi, just north of Mesa. We watched those chicks religiously, every hour for the first few days, and then closely thereafter until they feathered out and could be moved from their brooder house to a new 40-by-80-foot hen house that my folks had built.

We brooded a second group of 500 chicks as soon as the first 500 were safely nesting in their larger home. By the end of 1943, we had a total of 1,000 pullets (young hens) ready to lay eggs.

A year later, my parents had another hen house built, and they purchased two more 500-chick broods. It wasn't long before we had 2,000 laying hens. In the years to come, we also began brooding several hundred fryers. We would purchase them in the late summer, if the market looked like it might be lucrative come fall.

The two brooder houses were moved several years later to a plot of land north of Thomas Road, on the west side of Miller Road. They stood there until they were torn down in the mid-1990s.

Although they're gone now, they still remind me of how much I've enjoyed construction since I first helped build those brooder houses more than a half-century ago.

The Messinger family farm featured two brooder houses. They got into raising chickens in 1943, starting with 500 day-old leghorn chicks they purchased from a Lehi farmer north of Mesa. A year later, they had 2,000 laying hens. In addition to selling eggs, the family raised fryers. Building the family's first brooder house was Paul Messinger's first real construction experience.

LEVI'S WERE UNWRITTEN DRESS CODE FOR SCOTTSDALE HIGH BOYS

Scottsdale Republic, January 20, 2006

When I entered Scottsdale High School as a freshman in the fall of 1944, all of the boys wore Levi's jeans. We didn't wear Wranglers or 101s or any other make of denim pants. I don't know why that was the case.

Our mothers just knew that they couldn't send us to school with some other make of trousers.

Every fall, and this was true in 1944, boys who were new to the school and who didn't get the word on pants, often would wear another make of denims. It was standard practice to catch them, remove their denims and run them (their pants) up the school flagpole. This stunt wasn't popular with the school administration. Supposedly, the perpetrators of such pranks could be expelled. I don't remember anyone actually getting kicked out, however.

Although Levi's were hard to come by during World War II, that fact didn't change the unwritten rule. Boys would lend a friend a pair of theirs if that friend didn't have any or couldn't buy a pair.

We also wore our Levi's to Scottsdale High dances. They were held in the old "tin gymnasium" after football and basketball games.

Dances were different back then. We always had a live band. No one danced to records except, of course, when learning to dance at home. The bands usually consisted of three or four musicians. They played the pop tunes of the day.

Some of those songs my wife, Cora, still remembers. They included *In the Mood, Begin the Beguine, Night and Day, I Got a Gal in Kalamazoo, String of Pearls* and *Always*.

Parents often came to our dances and danced alongside their children. Sometimes they danced with their children or other students. Almost all of the dancing was ballroom-style, mostly two-step. A few did a basic type of jitterbugging, but it was very basic.

I can remember seeing young men out on the driveway in front of the gym, practicing their dancing with a parent or one of the girls. We farm kids weren't Don Juans.

Dress at these dances was, for boys, Levi's (as I mentioned), a clean shirt, a string tie, your best pair of polished cowboy boots and, usually, a tweed sport coat. This was considered formal attire. If it was early fall and still warm, we skipped the string tie and coat.

The girls wore what the boys called "curtain" dresses. They were ankle-length with a collar and puffed sleeves. They were made out of a material similar to home curtains. They, too, were the formal dress of that day. Some of the fellows usually went to Phoenix and purchased corsages for the rest of us to give to our girlfriends.

These dances were the social affairs at Scottsdale High and, quite often, the community at-large. We had a Sadie Hawkins Dance, where the girls would ask the boys, and a Sweetheart Dance in the spring, where we elected our annual king and queen. Sometimes, we held a Western dance. We would bring bales of hay to sit on while the country band played Western music.

Scottsdale High was small when I attended, roughly 100 students.

64

You knew everyone and most of their parents.

Dance bands cost $150 to $200 a night. Corsages were $2.50 to $3.00. The girls were happy if your dad let you use the farm pickup truck on your date.

Those were great days, and to this day, I still wear Levi's when I wear denim.

Boys at Scottsdale High School wore Levi's jeans in the 1940s, even for special school dances. Dance dress for the boys was Levi's, a clean shirt, a string tie, your best pair of polished cowboy boots and, usually, a tweed sport coat. Girls wore what the boys called "curtain" dresses, pretty ankle-length frocks with puffed sleeves that were made out of a material similar to home curtains. Here, Cora Ross (later Messinger) and Rusty Lyon reigned as royalty at a 1948 dance.

POST OFFICE ONCE GATHERING PLACE FOR SCOTTSDALE RESIDENTS

Scottsdale Republic, March 3, 2006

When I came to Scottsdale as a young boy in 1942, the town's post office was located on the lower floor of the two-story building where Porter's Western Store sits today, on Brown Street just north of Main Street.

Everyone had a post office box back then, or they received their mail via general delivery. Mr. Adams was the postmaster. Everyone knew him.

The post office was the gathering place for the entire community. I imagine this is true in many small towns today. When you went there, you inevitably ran into a broad cross section of people. It was a great place to spend a few minutes talking to neighbors and friends. It's where you learned all the local news.

People talked about who was getting married and what was happening at the high school. You discussed crops, world news and anything else you wanted to share or find out more about.

Savvy salesmen used to frequent the post office, too. I can remember my parents purchasing beef tamales and apples from people standing outside the post office door.

One evening, my dad and I drove over to pick up the mail. I ran inside to get it. When I came out, a fellow was standing next to our truck, talking to my dad (to whom he had given a cigar).

He was trying to sell him an acre of land near today's downtown. It had two small shacks that rented for $10 and $15 a month, respectively. He wanted $1,500 for the property. Always

polite, my dad listened to what the salesman had to say and then opined that he didn't want to be a landlord.

That didn't go over well. The salesman grabbed the cigar he'd given my dad and moved on to persuade someone else. I remember my dad laughing about the cigar, saying the salesman's choice of brands was rather poor. Today, the land that the man wanted to sell to my dad is sitting beneath the southern half of Pima Plaza (Old Town Plaza).

Also, back in the 1940s, if your parents were tired after a hard day at work, you often took the family pickup to go get the mail. Young people could legally drive when they were 14 years, 9 months of age.

One evening, when I was about 13 – granted, younger than the age requirement for driving– I sped off to the post office, stopping on a dime outside its front door, just as Al Frederick, Scottsdale's town constable, walked out that same door and into my formidable cloud of dust.

He strolled over to the driver's side of my dad's truck and said, "Would you like to try that again?" Needless to say, yes, I did.

I backed up slowly, drove around the block and made a point of parking very carefully when I returned. When I got out of the truck, Al said, "For a minute there, I thought I was going to have to check your license." Then, he walked away and drove off.

These days, some 64 years later, my wife, Cora, and I still have the same post office box. I check it once or twice a week. That said, going to the post office isn't the same as it used to be. We occasionally see a few long-time friends, but most of the people we meet are strangers.

Constable Al Frederick, who served in that capacity from the 1920s until his death in 1950, once caught an underage, 13-year-old Paul Messinger arriving by pickup truck at the post office in a cloud of dust. He didn't ticket the boy but did suggest he might "try that again," more slowly the second time. The Messingers have maintained the same post office box for 68 years.

AT LEAST ONE GAS STATION PROVIDED MORE THAN FUEL, SERVICE

Scottsdale Republic, April 28, 2006

At gasoline stations in the 1940s and the 1950s, either the proprietor or one of his attendants pumped gas for you. No customer ever thought of pumping his own gasoline.

When you pulled into the stations, your tank would be filled, the air pressure in your tires would be checked, as well as the water levels in your battery and the amount of oil in your engine. You also would get your windshield washed, and, if you asked, the rest of the windows washed, your brake fluid checked and your floor brushed out.

That's why they called them "service" stations back then. The services that one station provided were what differentiated it from another service station down the road. The price of gasoline varied from 15 cents to 25 cents a gallon.

In the 1930s, Ivy Avery began operating the "76" service station on the northwestern corner of Scottsdale and Thomas Roads. Although it was a company station, you would have thought Ivy owned it. He took that much pride in every service he provided, plus one additional service that most of his competitors didn't offer – he asked about your family and told you what was going on in Scottsdale.

By the time you left, you knew who was ailing and who was organizing a wonderful family event. In a most gracious way, he kept you informed. At the same time, he found out what was happening in your life.

Ivy wasn't a gossip. He provided a public service. The news and information he imparted gave support to those in need and made folks aware of special situations. His tact and the care he demonstrated were his hallmark.

In the late 1940s, Ivy built a Richfield service station on the southeastern corner of the same intersection. Ivy owned it, and he and his son, Burl, ran the station until the late 1980s. Today, a McDonald's restaurant sits on the site.

My most vivid memories are those of me and my parents pulling into the station to find cars backed up two-or-three-deep. Ivy, H.F. Croom, Mike Robbins and the other attendants could be seen performing every service imaginable, while bringing each driver up to date on what was happening in town. Everyone waited patiently because you knew that you would be treated just as well when your turn came.

It seems we had more time back then, to properly service our cars and share some news with a friend. I miss Ivy's special care and the friendly conversations we used to have.

I worked for Ivy for a few months, as did many other young Scottsdale men. Ivy taught his employees a host of lessons not found in management books. That's why, many years later, many of them went on to succeed in business themselves.

Ivy Avery operated service stations in Scottsdale from the 1930s to the late 1980s. Ivy not only provided outstanding customer service, but he was a reliable source of information about everything going on in the community.

IMMIGRANTS, FOREIGN AND DOMESTIC, SHAPED AREA AS WE KNOW IT

Scottsdale Republic, May 26, 2006

During World War II, Scottsdale welcomed people from everywhere.

Farmers began to arrive from such states as Mississippi, Oklahoma and Arkansas. Many moved here for a fresh start, having suffered at the hands of tremendous natural disasters. Back then, the damage and chaos of a storm of Hurricane Katrina's size had to be endured without the benefit of government aid.

At the same time, Mexican men were traveling to Arizona, looking for work. When they earned enough money, they generally returned to Mexico to grubstake farms or to take advantage of other business opportunities.

Meanwhile, thousands of American GIs were sent here to learn how to fly, or fix and maintain, military aircraft. Ironically, a large number of prisoners of war were housed here as well. Unlike the farmers and foreign workers, however, none of them came by choice.

The prisoners were put to work cleaning irrigation ditches and performing other jobs that needed to be done, while our own young people fought pitched battles overseas.

The new farmers spent their days growing food and fiber for a nation that badly needed both. They purchased land and planted or raised here what each had planted or raised back home. Those from the South grew cotton. Those from the Midwest concentrated on dairy cows, row crops and poultry.

Around this time, farm machinery was becoming increasingly popular. Because of the war, however, it was in short supply. To make matters worse, all physically fit young men were away in the service.

As such, workers from Mexico were welcomed with open arms. All of the men we knew, and those we worked with, had temporary papers and were in this country legally.

Generally speaking, during the war years, usually only men came up from Mexico to find work. After they had been here a few times, however, some brought their families back with them. All in all, people everywhere were experiencing great upheaval and each was just trying to survive.

That said, there was very little strife among these new faces, whether they were farmers, guest workers or captured foreign fighters.

When I first started traveling to Mexico in the 1950s, we often visited people who had worked here before returning home. It was during those years that the rivers on the western side of the Sierra Madre were dammed and irrigation canals were built. They fueled the fertile agricultural lands of Sonora and Sinaloa, farms that produce many of the vegetables that we eat today.

Word of this agricultural boom spread, and a lot of the workers who had come to Arizona returned to Mexico to join the region's pioneer farmers. They had a vision of what their country could become, and they got to work to make it happen.

Banks opened. Highways were built. In fact, Sonora and parts of Sinaloa developed in much the same way that the U.S. had developed. These trends continued through the 1960s,

1970s and the 1980s. Somehow, though, the area's agricultural prosperity didn't spread to the central and southern parts of the country.

Then, as now, too few Mexicans share in the fruits of their hard work.

During World War II, all physically fit American men were away in the service, and farm machinery was in short supply. Scottsdale welcomed Mexican immigrant workers, who at that time could enter the country legally and receive temporary papers allowing them to work in the United States.

CANAL SKIING WAS A 1940s ART FORM FOR DESERT DUDES

Scottsdale Republic, June 23, 2006

In the 1940s, water skiing on Scottsdale's section of the Arizona Canal was the buzz. Every teenage boy had his own idea of how best to ski the canal.

We built our ski boards out of plywood, sawing grooves on the top of the wood so we could bend the tip upward, just like a modern-day water ski. Then, we drilled holes in the board so a towrope could be tied to the board and then tied to a post on the back of a pickup truck.

Ropes were also attached to the front of the board. That way, you could stand on the board and lean backward, holding the ropes to balance and guide the board as it pulled you along the canal. In those days, the dirt roads next to the canal were open to the public. Today, they're private, used by Salt River Project employees to operate and maintain the canal.

There were many types of ski boards. Some had round fronts. Others had square fronts. A few had curved metal fronts. One fellow used the hood of an old car!

Rather than tie the towrope to their boards, some canal skiers were pulled by a hand rope. The skier held on to the towrope and let go of it if the ride got out of control. It was a little safer to do it that way, but less likely to give you a good ride. As I remember, most boards were tied to the back of the "pulling" truck. You had a lot less control, but a lot more fun.

In any case, every half-mile or so there usually was a road over the canal. Your ride ended at each bridge and had to be restarted on the other side.

Riding a ski board pulled by a truck took some special skills. Because the truck ran alongside the canal, it tended to pull you toward the bank of the canal. You had to lean away from the bank in order to go straight.

Being "desert kids," we had to learn to ride a ski board from scratch. It wasn't easy because no one knew how it was supposed to be done. Nonetheless, although we had no ocean for practice, we had some good rides and gained a crude level of skill. Lord knows we certainly gave it enough effort.

Rather than use a truck, a few guys tried pulling their ski boards with a horse. They had little success. It took a fair amount of coordination and a lot more than "horse power" to pull a ski board along an irrigation canal.

I don't remember anyone ever getting more than a scrape or a bruise while water skiing on the Arizona Canal. In retrospect, it doesn't seem like a safe thing to do.

Presumably, that's why the folks at SRP don't allow canal skiing today. Bill Schrader, the company's former president, probably had some special insights into the pro's and con's of canal skiing. He was, after all, a local young man of that era.

Because canal skiing was not a sanctioned sport endorsed by parents, police or water officials, there don't seem to be any pictures of canal skiing in Scottsdale. One of the canals' most important purposes was to provide irrigation water to local farmers. Here, George Ellis and his son, David, are pictured next to an irrigation ditch carrying water to their land.

LOVE OF CLASSIC CARS IS CONDITION THAT DOESN'T DISSIPATE WITH AGE

Scottsdale Republic, August 4, 2006

If you were a teenager or older from 1945 to 1950 and living in Scottsdale or most other small towns, you can appreciate the many opportunities we had to get our hands dirty working on cars and practicing our fledgling mechanical skills.

Back then, most farms had workshops filled with tools. If not, you had a connection with a local repair garage or gas station. Because World War II limited the production of new cars, those built in the 1920s, '30s and early '40s had been driven more miles than would have normally been the case. As such, you could purchase one of those cars for very few dollars.

The combination of readily available and affordable cars, all manner of tools and the money we boys earned from our natural hard-working nature made it almost a crime not to build a hot rod.

Thanks to my parents, I got the chance to work on several old cars of my own. Unfortunately, I didn't get as many chances to test-drive those cars as I wanted.

One of my favorites was our 1919 Model "T" Ford. We dropped the front and rear transverse springs by having Dunbar Spring Company modify them. We put a Delco Remy distributor on the engine, shaved the head, changed carburetors, put on exhaust headers and used a Buick drive shaft housing with a Smitty muffler for the exhaust pipe.

We removed the fenders and most of the body, but not the windshield, dashboard, front doors or front seat. The car was fast up to 85 mph. Then, its speed pretty much flattened out. We had four other Model Ts, some obtained mostly in parts, a few pieces at a time.

Friends of mine like Dwaune Howard, Bill McKinsey and Norman Wolf were more creative. They had real cars.

Both Dwaune and Bill had 1932 Ford V-8 Model "B" hot rods. They had flat-head engines running Edelbrock heads as well as dual ignition systems, chrome headers, dual carburetors and more. They pulled off the fenders, lowered the springs, put motorcycle tires on the front and big wheels and tires on the back.

The car bodies were ragtop coupes with a rumble seat and leather tucked-and-rolled upholstery. These cars really ran fast. They may well have exceeded speeds of 125 mph. After all, they could go over 85 mph in second gear! They were beautiful cars just to see, let alone drive.

Norman Wolf was an auto driver for *The Arizona Republic* in 1945. He had a low-slung Plymouth with a dual Smitty exhaust system and further modifications under the hood. He never opened the hood to show us. Instead, he let his car do his talking. I sure loved to hear that car pass by.

Many young men of that era owned and modified all kinds of older cars. You would have to write a book to do justice to the subject.

For example, Bill Schrader had a fancy Ford Model "T." The Hardison brothers had a 1932 Rockne coupe (a Studebaker product) and Gib McFarland had a six-cylinder Star car.

This is just a partial list of the local hot rod enthusiasts of my boyhood.

To this day, I still enjoy going to the Pavilions shopping center in north Scottsdale on Saturday night to see the cars that men and boys enjoy today.

If you've read this far, you're probably a car buff like me. Loving these cars is a terminal disease, one that's tough to keep in remission.

Scottsdale boys in the 1940s liked to build or modify their own hot rods. Dwaune Howard and Bill McKinsey owned 1932 Ford Model B V-8s like the one pictured here. Dwaune and Bill pulled off the fenders, lowered the springs, put motorcycle tires on the front and big wheels and tires on the backs of their cars.

BENEVOLENT CIVIL SERVANTS PAVED ROAD TO HAPPINESS

Scottsdale Republic, November 23, 2006

In 1950, two 20-year-olds wanted to marry each other. They selected Thanksgiving Day because neither of them had to go to work.

In the wee hours of that November 23rd morning, they drove down to Florence. Back then, it was a popular place to get married. When the happy couple got to the Pinal County courthouse, they used a flashlight to read the sign to check when it would open.

The sign on the door read: "Open Monday to Friday, 8 to 5." That was a good thing, because Thanksgiving Day fell on a Thursday. They waited patiently in their car in front of the courthouse. The sun came up, and 8:00 a.m. finally arrived. Then 8:15 a.m. Unfortunately, no one arrived to open the door.

The young man walked around the side of the building and down into the basement where he found the Pinal County Sheriff's Office. The deputy told him that the courthouse wouldn't be open that day because it was Thanksgiving. The deputy gave the young man the Pinal County Clerk's home telephone number and offered him the use of a telephone.

The groom-to-be called the clerk, who agreed to come down to the courthouse. He met the young couple in front of the building. They walked up to a big office on the second floor.

The clerk opened a walk-in safe and came back with a marriage license. He filled it out, and the couple paid him the required $5 fee. The young man then said, "I suppose the Justice of the Peace isn't coming in, either." The clerk concurred but said that the Justice of the Peace in nearby Coolidge was on-call.

The couple felt their plight qualified as an emergency, so they drove to Coolidge and found Justice of the Peace T.M. Hagee. The judge said he would marry them if they waited until he finished mowing his lawn. The wedding was held in Hagee's living room, a little before noon on Thanksgiving Day. Mrs. Hagee and Miss Mary Sue Hagee served as witnesses.

My wife, Cora, and I know this story well, because we were that couple, the two who got hitched on Thanksgiving Day back in 1950. I have a lot to be thankful for, as do all of us who have been fortunate enough to meet, marry and love a lifelong partner.

In 1950, Paul and Cora Messinger decided to get married on Thanksgiving Day because it was a day when neither of them had to work. They drove to Florence to get the license and then on to Coolidge, where Pinal County Justice of the Peace T.M. Hagee performed the wedding.

IN DAYS GONE BY, EARNING 'SPURS' WAS HONEST MEASURE OF A PERSON

Scottsdale Republic, February 2, 2007

One of my favorite memories in a funeral service is the rosaries that we held during the late 1950s and early 1960s.

There was a practice roping arena on the northern side of Indian School Road, across the street from our mortuary. Yale Siminoff operated the arena. It consisted of a big fenced arena, a calf chute for releasing calves and an open-sided pen so the cowboy ropers could bolt into the arena and give chase.

The soil in the arena was kept soft by regular discing or harrowing. That kept it loose. This provided good traction, making it easier for the chase horses to dig in their hoofs and keep the calf rope tight, once the cowboy had successfully lassoed the calf.

There were floodlights, so the cowboys could practice roping and tying calves in the evenings prior to rodeo events. In those days, rodeos were held in Chandler, the Salt River Indian Reservation, Phoenix, Scottsdale, Wickenburg, Payson and Prescott, and many other towns.

On evenings when our mortuary held a Catholic rosary service, the men in attendance could often be found standing on the mortuary porch, looking across the street, watching and timing the ropers. A calf came out of the chute every three to five minutes.

As the rosaries were about to begin, the late Father Eugene Maguire, long-time pastor of Our Lady of Perpetual Help Catholic Church that was located next door, would ask me to get the men off the porch and into the chapel.

I would tell them, "It's time to come in for the rosary." They would answer, "One more calf." Then, once I had successfully herded them into our chapel and we were ready to start, I had to find Father Maguire (who, by this time, was often on the porch!). With his great sense of humor, he would say, "One more calf."

The nearby arena caused more than distractions. When the wind blew from the northeast, we endured all manner of blowing dirt and manure. A few times it was so bad that we couldn't see across the two lanes of Indian School Road. We had to put masking tape around our front door to keep the dirt and other stuff out of our front lobby.

Today, unlike the 1950s, most people turn to government to enforce nuisance ordinances. Back then, you protected yourself and tried your dead-level best not to interfere with your neighbor.

Furthermore, because we were located in Scottsdale, and the rodeo arena was located in an unincorporated portion of Maricopa County, we were never sure whether the land adjacent to the intersection of Miller and Indian School Roads was rural or municipal. In other words, to whom would we have complained if we had wanted to?

Rodeos were important back then, so much so that schools would end the day early so that students could attend them. County sheriffs were elected by how well they competed at local "sheriffs" rodeos. Every town took pride in its local rodeos, just as we did at our own rodeo.

Earning your "spurs" in those days was a measure of your character, strength and backbone.

Scottsdale took its rodeos very seriously. In the late 1950s and early 1960s, there was a practice roping arena on the north side of Indian School, across the street from Messinger Mortuary.

LONG AGO, SMELLS THAT FILLED THE VALLEY WERE PLEASANT, NOT FOUL

Scottsdale Republic, February 19, 2007

Sixty years ago, when it rained, we could smell the distant and distinctive scent of the desert. It blanketed downtown Scottsdale.

It was a peculiar smell, a combination of the dust on greasewood (creosote bushes) mixed with rainwater. When you took in a deep breath, you felt good - because rainfall in Arizona is always good.

Back then, if you had lived here long enough, the smell was ingrained into your memories of familiar scents. It foretold the coming of rain. The birds and small animals seemed to scurry for cover when gentle winds swept that odor across the desert floor.

I also remember the smell of newly mowed hay. Alfalfa and clover have a mildly sweet scent. If you were driving past a field where the hay had just been cut, the odor would immediately grab your attention. The fertile land and temperate Scottsdale weather allowed farmers to harvest six to eight cuttings of hay from the same field each year.

Once cut, the hay dried quickly. If the hay was cut in the morning, it needed to be baled before dark. There was a lot of work for local high school boys charged with moving the hay out of the field as fast as it was baled. Speed was important because the farmers wanted to irrigate immediately so they could cut more hay in three or four weeks.

Another nostalgic smell was the odor of the earth rolling over as you plowed it. Sharp disc blades cut deep into the dirt, shredding roots and churning the rich topsoil. That's how you prepared your field for the next crop.

In this regard, Arizona's sandy loam soil had a special scent. If your nose was willing, it didn't take much to soak up its full aroma. As an aside, and as a mortician, I've always been struck by the fact that people find comfort when they return their loved ones to the Earth.

A farm smell that many of my urban friends might find discomforting is that of manure combined with the earth. Cattle manure dries quickly in these parts, and its aroma creates a truly unique odor. Need I say more? Most "city folks" consider the scent foul. But, I've heard many a cattleman say, "It smells like money!"

One smell we no longer experience today is that of the "smudge pots" that used to dot citrus groves. On cold nights, when the temperature dropped into the mid-20s, farmers would burn oil in iron containers in order to keep their west Scottsdale and Arcadia citrus trees from freezing.

They also would trickle irrigation water through the groves, or use large fans, to soften the cold. The smoke from the smudge pots often mixed with the fog coming off the water under the citrus trees.

While there are still plenty of citrus trees with fragrant seasonal blossoms, few locals raise fruit for a living. Today, we put up with the smells of vehicle exhaust, tobacco smoke and industrial odors.

To those who were raised in the hearts of major cities, I hope these reminiscences of rural smells remind you of others, of times and adventure that warm your hearts. It's great to smell the roses, wherever you come from.

Newly mowed hay was one of the wonderful smells when Scottsdale still had farms. If you were driving past a field where the hay had just been cut, the odor would immediately grab your attention. If hay was cut in the morning, it needed to be baled by dark. High school boys found work moving the hay out of the fields as fast as it was baled so farmers could irrigate immediately and cut more hay in three or four weeks.

SHALLER LAND PLAYED ROLE IN CITY'S GROWTH

Scottsdale Republic, March 30, 2007

For farmers, most measurements are based on an acre of land. What's called a "section" is one square mile in size. A "quarter" section contains 160 acres, or four units of land comprised of 40 acres each. Each side of what's termed a "40" is a quarter-mile long.

The 40-acre "quarter-quarter" section, which extended west from our family farm and across Miller Road toward today's Civic Center Mall, belonged to Stanley Shaller. In 1942, he raised alfalfa hay on it and lived in a house that sat where the intersection of Miller Road and Main Street sits today.

In the mid 1940s, he sold his land to C.B. Reddell. C.B. raised watermelons and cantaloupes on it for four to five years and then sold the land to a home developer named Hinton.

Hinton put in Hinton Road (today's 74th Street) running from Indian School Road south to Second Street. He built frame homes on the west 20 acres of the 40-acre parcel, between George Street (later Civic Center Plaza and now Drinkwater Boulevard) and Hinton Road.

A fellow named Scotty Martin purchased a single acre of Hinton's property on the northwestern corner of his subdivision. He built a swimming pool and a restaurant.

It was Scottsdale's first public swimming pool. He operated the pool for four years, but had continual problems with the Maricopa County Health Department over the pool's water temperature. He couldn't keep the water cool enough, and he eventually sold the property.

Later on, the site was turned into a small bowling alley. After that it became Ford Theater. Neither was successful. Today, Scottsdale's "One Stop Shop" complex sits on the site.

Around 1947, simple homes made of concrete block were built on 10 acres on the southeastern corner of the old Shaller parcel. Many of those homes are still standing. Then, in 1949, a developer named LaMar purchased the northeastern 10 acres and built more elaborate concrete block homes.

They were three bedrooms with one bathroom and an evaporative cooler. They sold for $6,995, with a down payment of $395. The homes were financed by the Equitable Insurance Co. at 4.78 percent interest. The payments were $48.35 a month.

At the time, we thought the homes were a little pricey. But, 20 years later, after the price had inflated to almost $20,000 each, we bought two of them. They still had mortgages. We paid $48.35 a month on each until both homes were paid off.

The little curved road called Redel Street (Redell Avenue on some of today's maps, Reddell on others), which runs through the LaMar development from Miller Road to Indian School Road, was named for C.B. Reddell. City workers shortened his name to "Redel" so it would fit on the street sign!

Another road, McNight Street (now Avenue), was named after Bob McNight. He was the civil engineer who laid out LaMar's subdivision plat. At one time, McNight was married to Murle

Miller. She was the daughter of Charles Miller, for whom Miller Road is named.

In the early 1970s, Scottsdale purchased the western 20 acres of the 40-acre parcel originally owned by Stanley Shaller from the families that owned the Hinton-built frame homes. That's where our City Hall and main library now stand. I use the word "purchased" because the sale of the land was gained through negotiation and not through condemnation.

Just think. This land has been in active use serving its owners (Shaller, Reddell, Martin, Hinton, LaMar and the city) and the community in general for more than 100 years. To this day, it's still gradually changing to meet the needs of new owners and the citizens of Scottsdale.

Simple three bedroom, one bath concrete block homes were constructed in the late forties on the old Shaller farm land, west of Miller near today's Civic Center Mall. Until recently, this home was owned by Bill Schrader.

WALKING, WORKING, EATING RIGHT KEPT '40s KIDS TRIM

Scottsdale Republic, August 3, 2007

When I was a boy, in the 1930s and 1940s, everyone in Scottsdale walked everywhere. We walked to school, down the lane to bring the cows up for milking and to neighboring farms. Sometimes, we went for a walk for the sake of taking a walk.

We didn't have walking shoes or running shoes back then. The tennis shoes of that era were made of rubber and canvas. There were high-top versions and the low ones as well. A lot of us wore U.S. Keds. Most tennis shoes didn't breathe very well. They were mainly used for sports like tennis, baseball and basketball.

In those years, we didn't see the number of overweight young people or adults that we see today. People ate a lot of meat and potatoes, much more gravy and probably less salad when I was a boy. However, we had vegetables at dinner every night and bread was apportioned by the slice. We didn't drink much soda pop, but what we did drink usually came in 8-ounce bottles (although Pepsi kept bragging about its new 12-ounce bottles).

We ate far fewer sandwiches, and considering how big hamburger and other buns are today, we probably ate a lot less starch. Breakfast was usually the major meal of the day. Dinners were smaller and well balanced.

What's different today from yesterday that causes so many people to be overweight? Well, for one thing, these days everyone uses a car to travel as few as one or two blocks. Young people use bicycles or hit their folks up for a ride.

While we weren't any smarter in my youth, we were definitely used to walking. You could then (and still can today) walk a couple of miles in 30 minutes or a mile in less time. When we walked, we didn't have to wait for our moms to get ready, get the car out and take us where we wanted to go. Walking got us to our destinations just as quickly and gave us a lot more independence.

Additionally, we didn't have television. Radio was our principal form of entertainment. Still, we rarely listened to programs that were longer than 30 minutes, shows like *The Lone Ranger*. Many programs, like *Tom Mix* and *The Green Hornet*, were only 15 minutes long. As such, we didn't spend a lot of time sitting around.

We also had physical education courses in Scottsdale's schools. That said, I don't think we got much education. For example, if you milked cows like I did, you got out of high school one hour early and you got credit for physical education for doing your milking. Not much education there.

In the end, however, we kept our weight down. That made us feel more energetic and, as a result, we tended to pursue more physical activity. We played backyard football, baseball and basketball. We also tossed the ball with our friends, our dads or our brothers in the evening. I don't see much of that happening today.

We were lucky to grow up in Scottsdale when we did. Our meals were well balanced.

Exercise was the thing to do. The more pervasive use of wheels and television were still looming on the horizon.

Today, in Scottsdale and elsewhere, weight is a genuine hazard facing our young people. I hope this generation will solve that problem. However, assuming it gets settled, you can't help but wonder what will come next.

In the 1930s and '40s, you didn't see a lot of overweight kids in Scottsdale. That's because they had tons of chores to do and they walked everywhere – to school and back, to bring the cows in, to take the cows out. Here, Philip Messinger is pictured doing his milking chores on the Messinger family farm and dairy.

YOUNG FUNERAL DIRECTOR ONCE HAD TO GET DOWN AND DIRTY

Scottsdale Republic, September 28, 2007

In 1957, the Phoenix-based mortuary where I worked (before I opened my own mortuary in Scottsdale) was asked to handle funeral services for the much-loved former Town Clerk of Tombstone, Arizona. I was the funeral director in charge, responsible for managing the arrangements and subsequent service.

Because of the travel distance involved (more than 150 miles south of Phoenix) and given my lack of familiarity with Tombstone, I decided to leave early on the day of the scheduled service. I asked my wife Cora to come along with me.

As was the custom in small towns in Arizona at that time, the funeral director was expected to provide a rough box to hold the casket when the deceased was put to rest. The box was put in the grave first. Then, the casket was placed inside the box, which was supposed to keep the earth from coming into direct contact with the casket.

In order to transport both the box and the casket in the funeral coach, we put the casket inside the rough box and put the rough box inside the coach. When you did it that way you had to go to the cemetery first, unload the box, remove the casket, put the box in the grave and put the casket back in the coach. From there you drove the casket to the church where the service was going to be held.

In this particular case, when we got to the grave site in a little cemetery west of town, we found that the gravedigger had dug a hole about 2 feet deep. His shovel was still there. He was gone.

When we arrived at the church, we arranged the casket, along with dozens of bouquets of flowers. It was still four hours until the early afternoon ceremony would begin.

Cora continued setting up the flowers and preparing the church for the pending visitation while I called the Town of Tombstone to inquire about the unfinished grave. They said they had paid the gravedigger to dig the grave and surmised he had downed a few too many drinks the night before and forgotten to finish it. In other words, I was on my own.

There I stood, in a black suit, a white shirt and a tie next to a partially dug grave.

I was a young man with only one option. I would have to finish digging the grave myself. I took off my shirt and tie, rolled up my pant legs and grabbed the shovel. In two hours I had the grave fully dug and the rough box set inside.

When I got back to the church, the pastor's wife let me take a shower in the rectory. While I was doing that, she and Cora beat the dirt out of my pants and pressed them.

We conducted the service on time for an overflow crowd. After it was over, local florists hauled the flowers to the cemetery. The funeral procession was so long (and the Town of Tombstone so small) that cars were still leaving the church by the time the coach and the casket arrived at the cemetery.

After a graveside service, we lowered the casket into the rough box and closed it. The now-sober gravedigger returned to the cemetery and filled the grave. We left Tombstone and got back to our home in Scottsdale about 9 o'clock that evening, roughly 18 hours after we had left town.

Needless to say, we were tired. But, we were also very satisfied. After all, we had worked through the difficult burial of a real Arizona pioneer, Nellie Dalgish, Tombstone's Town Clerk for nearly half a century.

When Paul Messinger was given the responsibility for managing the funeral service and burial for former Tombstone Town Clerk Nellie Dalgish, he arrived in Tombstone with the casket and the burial box only to find that the gravedigger had quit before finishing the grave. In a black suit, starched white shirt and tie, Paul had no option other than to finish digging the grave himself. He finished the job in two hours and then showered at the rectory at St. Paul's Episcopal Church prior to the service.

St. Paul's Episcopal Church is the oldest Protestant church in Arizona still standing on its earliest site with original stained glass and elegant lighting fixtures that came from a 19th century whaling ship.

PHILIPPINES APPRECIATIVE OF U.S. SOLDIERS' EFFORTS

Scottsdale Republic, December 7, 2007

An attorney, Fred Morton Raymond, who had been a partner in the law firm where my father started practicing, was appointed a federal judge for western Michigan in 1929. Among the first official duties he was faced with was the prospect of sending a young boy from the Philippines back to his home on Occidental Mindoro Island.

The boy's uncle in the United States had died. Another sponsor would have to be found if he was to remain in the US. Judge Raymond, whose last name was given to me as my middle name, asked my parents if they would consider sponsoring the boy. They agreed to accept sponsorship of Reynaldo R. Curva. He graduated from law school and passed the Michigan Bar in the fall of 1941.

Later that fall, on December 7, 1941, the Japanese attacked Pearl Harbor. They also attacked the Philippines, which aroused Rey's deepest patriotic feelings. He joined the U.S. Army.

In the Army, because of his education, his ethnic background and because he could speak the dialect of his native island, he was placed in an Army intelligence unit. We didn't hear from him after that. It was only after the Philippines were retaken that we learned why we had lost contact with him and why we hadn't received any letters from Rey.

As it turned out, Rey had been dropped by parachute near San Jose, Occidental Mindoro, his birthplace, about 250 miles southwest of Manila. He was accompanied by another U.S. soldier of Philippine descent. They had a radio.

Their mission was to keep U.S. armed forces informed of significant military matters.

They developed contacts with local citizens, the people who became their eyes and ears on the ground. Then, at specific times, they went into the mountains, high above the ocean, and radioed coded messages to nearby submarines, which would surface at night in the South China Sea for the purpose of receiving their periodic reports.

As soon as the radio transmissions were completed, the submarine and Rey and his partner had to get as far away, and as quickly as possible, to prevent the Japanese from triangulating the location of the source of the radio messages as well as the location of the submarine. Rey's isolation prevented him from contacting us.

Merle Dahn, a mortician with Messinger Indian School Mortuary from 1976 to 2006, died in the fall of 2007. He was a Bosen's Mate on a submarine that worked the South China Sea in and around the Philippine Islands during World War II.

He remembered surfacing on many nights to receive the kinds of radio messages that I've described. We have little doubt that Merle's submarine actually received Rey's radio transmissions. The time period involved and the locations of each were a match.

And, ironically, that's not the only match! After the war, a young woman named Inday, who was one of Rey's local contacts in San Jose, became Magdalena C. Curva, Rey's wife of almost 50 years.

After their marriage, Rey remained in the Philippines. He practiced law and taught part-time at a nearby college. He and Inday had five children, all of whom immigrated to the United States.

Rey died in 1995. Inday died in November 2007 (barely a month ago). Both are buried in San Jose.

My wife, Cora, and I have been to San Jose. While we were there, we spent time with Rey and Inday and are still in contact with their children today.

Mindoro was liberated shortly after Leyte Island. Rey showed us the various beachheads where American troops first hit the sand. There was Orange Beach and Blue Beach and countless other beaches. All are still marked.

We walked those hallowed grounds and visited the American Military Cemetery in Manila. It was truly the most beautiful cemetery of its kind that we have ever seen.

You can never appreciate the great admiration that the Philippine people have for America and for our soldiers unless you have an opportunity to travel there. We were so privileged.

Reynaldo R. Curva, a Philippine native pictured here with his wife Inday (Magdalena C. Curva), was living with the Messinger family in Michigan when Pearl Harbor and the Philippines were attacked in 1941. He volunteered for the Army and worked covertly in an intelligence unit monitoring enemy military movements in the Philippines.

It wasn't until many years later that the Messinger family learned that Merle Dahn (pictured below), a mortician with Messinger Indian School Mortuary from 1976 to 2006, was on the receiving end of Rey's radio transmissions when Dahn worked on a submarine in the South China Sea.

TRADITION BEGAN WITH LIFE-SIZE NATIVITY SCENE

Scottsdale Republic, December 21, 2007

In the fall of 1959, the portion of Indian School Road that ran in front of our newly built mortuary was two lanes wide. There was a major irrigation ditch along the south side and no curbs or streetlights on either side. At night, it was a dark stretch of rural road. With the mortuary's first Christmas coming up a few months hence, things seemed pretty bare for the holidays.

A few years earlier I had been working in Fontana, California, where we cut out a Santa figure from a sheet of structural board and painted it. All lit up, the Santa standing in our Fontana front yard looked great.

Now, having moved back to Scottsdale, we wondered whether we could build an entire Nativity scene. Since our newly established mortuary was too new to be very busy, we had plenty of time to devote to the project. The real question was whether we had enough talent and fortitude to do it right.

We purchased nine 4-by-8-foot sheets of structural board, painting one side white and the other side black. Then, we shot close-up color slides of as many nativity characters as we could find in various books and the Bible.

We projected the images from the slides onto the white sides of the structural board.

Our next step was to purchase paint. The outlines of the projected images were our guide. When necessary, we mixed different paints to get the shades we needed, but didn't have.

It took an evening or two to complete each figure. Within a month, we finished 14 life-size color images.

As it turned out, the irrigation ditch running along the south side of Indian School kept curious people from walking into the display. That was an important consideration because the baling wire we used to keep the figures standing upright was difficult to see at night. We didn't want people to trip over it and injure themselves.

For light, we made 10 wooden tripods and covered them with tar paper, leaving one side open. We put flood lights under the tripods and used the open ends to illuminate the site.

Because it was the only visible light along Indian School Road, it stood out and received a lot of public attention. Each Christmas thereafter, for another 10 years, we set up our colorful nativity display.

In 1969, my sister Mary Kitagawa and her family decided to move to Tucson. I gave her the nativity figures for use in her new neighborhood, a part of town that prided itself on its tradition of extensive Christmas decorations.

Years later, Mary moved to Amherst, Massachusetts, leaving the nativity scene with the people who purchased her Tucson home. What they did with it, I don't know.

But, this I do know. It was a challenging project and a wonderful tradition that brought our entire family together for the Christmas holidays.

It's in that spirit that my wife, Cora, and I wish you and yours a merry Christmas and a happy holiday season.

To celebrate Messinger Indian School Mortuary's first Christmas in 1959, the family built a complete nativity scene out of 4-by-8-foot sheets of structural board. Within a month, they finished 14 life-size images upon which they projected color slides of nativity characters. The nativity scene was featured at the mortuary for 10 years.

FLIGHT SCHOOL OPENED WORLD TO YOUNG PILOTS

Scottsdale Republic, February 1, 2008

In 1949, when I was a student at Phoenix College, I decided I wanted to learn to fly and get a private pilot's license.

No flying lessons were taught in Scottsdale. Today's Scottsdale Airpark was just an old training field left over from World War II.

Phoenix College, however, had opened a flight school at today's Phoenix Sky Harbor International Airport. They staffed it with instructors and several airplanes. Most were Aeronca Cubs. One was an Aeronca Chief.

Back then, Sky Harbor had one runway. A few shops, the flight school and a small public terminal with an aircraft control room (a control tower of sorts) sat on a strip of land north of the runway.

Before you could begin flying, you had to take courses on the theory of flight. Topics ranged from navigation and the study of weather to the dynamics of flight and the federal laws regulating private aviation.

You had to master these classes before the instructors would let you get in an airplane. It wasn't until we completed our classroom training that we got our flight logs, using them to track where we flew, the dates we flew and the number of hours we spent in the air.

A fellow named Bruce Bethancourt was my first flight instructor. The first flight we took together lasted 50 minutes. We flew over the Northeast Valley, Red Mountain, Fort McDowell, up to Pinnacle Peak, back over Scottsdale (where I circled around my parent's farm) and then back to Sky Harbor. You could see for miles. It was a thrill I remember to this day, one that occurred over 60 years ago!

Initially, students put in eight hours of dual flight time with their instructors. They taught us all sorts of "hands-on" maneuvers.

After that, we took the planes up solo, flying into designated airspace and practicing what we'd been taught. This included spins, stalls and making 360-degree turns (where the pilot had to keep the airplane's wingtip lined up with a point on the ground without a gain or loss of altitude). Although some of it was tedious, my flight skills and feel for flying gradually improved.

It wasn't too long before I had logged 32 hours of mixed solo and dual flight time (in addition to my initial 8 hours of flight). Some of those hours included cross country trips from Phoenix to Gila Bend, to Gilpin Field in Tucson and back to Phoenix or flights from Phoenix to Casa Grande and other small towns. Flight time, whether it was dual or solo, cost $3 an hour. Today, it costs many times that amount.

Those who were around the Valley in the late 1940s and early '50s probably remember the yellow Aeronca planes, with Phoenix College's bear logo on their sides, flying in and out of Sky Harbor dozens of times a day. Because there were so few commercial flights, we were allowed to practice touch-and-go landings and takeoffs on the airport's main runway. Today, many major airports have banned private aviation altogether.

Looking back, I take a lot of pride in the excellent training I received, training conducted by seasoned instructors using a well-maintained fleet of Aeronca airplanes.

Those years were a steppingstone in local flight history, when more and more civilians began flying and Sky Harbor has grown to be one of the busiest and most modern airports in the world.

Paul Messinger received his pilot's training in 1949 while a student at Phoenix College. After many hours of classroom training, the Phoenix College "Bear" took his first flight with instructor Bruce Bethancourt guiding him. Flight time in those days cost only $3 per hour. This photo from the 1950 Phoenix College Sandprints annual shows two students from that era.

LIVING IN SCOTTSDALE LETS US KEEP LINKS TO NATURE

Scottsdale Republic, June 27, 2008

I often think back to the 1940s when I was a boy growing up on our Scottsdale family farm, a 20-acre parcel at the southwest corner of Miller and Indian School Roads. It was rural, home to all sorts of birds, animals and other desert creatures. The houses were thinly spread, which meant you could hunt quail and doves freely.

Dove hunting usually started on the first Friday in September. If you forgot about it, the steady, early morning boom of shotguns reminded you. We hunted doves behind our milking barn, often standing in the irrigation ditch where Julio's Restaurant sits today.

We didn't hunt coyotes around the farm, but they were there. We had a 6-foot tall fence around our turkey and chicken runs to keep them from making a meal out of our poultry.

A full-grown coyote can get over a 6-foot wall. They generally jump on top of the wall and then into the enclosure. But a coyote can't land on top of a wire fence, and I've never seen one try.

As downtown Scottsdale became more densely populated, the coyotes moved farther north. Their lives seemed quite compatible with single-acre residential zoning. They had plenty of birds, small rodents, rabbits and the occasional open garbage can from which to choose. The coyotes were resourceful critters as people with pets often found out the hard way.

My wife, Cora, and I still see coyotes around our Scottsdale home, mostly in the early morning and late evening hours when they're hunting for food or searching for water. We've learned to live with them and enjoy their occasional night calls.

We also enjoy the company of a couple of different kinds of owls. When sitting outdoors, it's interesting to listen to the sounds they make trying to attract a rabbit, rodent or other small animal.

The owls make several kinds of sounds. One is a "click click" sound. Another is a whistle. A third is the familiar "who who." There are others.

They make their sounds and then sit quietly for a minute or so. When they spot their prey, they're quick to attack. A couple of years ago, we were caring for an ill swan in our backyard. One night, an owl killed it.

We also see our fair share of javalina wandering up and down   , north of Shea Boulevard. They seem to thrive in areas dominated by one-acre residential zoning.

Last summer we looked out our front window and saw seven javalina standing on our front porch. We have to keep our garage door closed so they don't eat all our grass seed.

Cora and I enjoy living in a community where nature is valued and respected and folks understand the do's and don'ts of living among the desert dwellers that eked out their livelihoods long before any of us urban pioneers arrived.

We can sit on our swing, smell the fresh air, listen to nature and watch the desert unfold before us. It's much less violent than today's television or the movies.

Scottsdale residents share their city with all manner of wildlife, including coyotes, rabbits, owls and even families of javalina that will sneak into your garage and steal your grass seed if you don't remember to keep the garage door closed.

MANY OF CITY'S REVERED STREET NAMES SURVIVE

Scottsdale Republic, July 25, 2008

Main Street and Scottsdale Roads used to serve as the "zero" points for establishing north-south and east-west addresses in Scottsdale. They were where our street numbers began.

For example, if you lived east of Scottsdale Road on Main Street your address could be 122 E. Main St. However, if you lived west of Scottsdale Road the corresponding address would be 122 W. Main St. Way back when Scottsdale was only a few blocks wide, our mortuary was at 515 E. Indian School Road. I used to live at 117 N. Miller Road.

In the late 1960s, Scottsdale's city fathers decided to extend the street numbering system used by Phoenix into Scottsdale. As such, the north-south and east-west "zero" points were moved. (Tempe and Mesa never adopted the Phoenix street numbering system.)

East-west street numbering now started at Central Avenue. All of a sudden, Messinger Mortuary's address became 7601 E. Indian School (no longer 515). Simultaneously, Washington became the new north-south "zero" point. Overnight, my home address became 4017 N. Miller Road (not 117).

Street names became another hurdle in this address nightmare. Mayor Bud Tims appointed Vice Mayor Ken Murray to head a citizens' committee to tackle the details. Which street names would remain the same and which ones would change?

The burning questions of that day were many: Should Orange become 68th Street? Should Miller Road become 76th Street?

I served on the committee. Those of us who opposed the name changes were able to keep these and other street names that reflected moments and people that made up the fabric of our local history.

We saved Brown Street, named for E. O. Brown; Miller Road, named for Charles Miller; Hayden Road, named for Wilford and Mittie Hayden; and Granite Reef Road, which was one of the streets you traveled on your way to Granite Reef Dam.

We also kept MacDonald Drive, named for Duncan MacDonald (which has since been shortened to McDonald).

We saved some roads because they had interesting names. Others were saved because mountains and other impediments prevented them from extending into Phoenix.

Years later, when city planners like George Fretz and Bill Walton were laying out McCormick Ranch (a newly proposed 5,000-acre-plus residential subdivision), many new street names were introduced.

Cadena was named for Benny Cadena. Other new street names included San Ramos, San Richardo and San Pedro. Farther north came hundreds of new roads. Some were rather colorfully named like Dynamite, Rusty Spur, Raintree, Evening Glow and Morning Breeze Drive.

Years later, city leaders found a street without a name. They decided to call it Murray Lane, honoring Scottsdale Vice Mayor Ken Murray, who took on the daunting task of adapting

Scottsdale's streets to the Phoenix address system. It's one block long, running off Miller Road along the northern side of Eldorado Park.

Ever wondered how Scottsdale streets got their names? In many cases, streets are named after early families who distinguished themselves through leadership and community service. Brown Avenue is named for E.O. Brown, whose son E.E. Brown is pictured here on horseback. Hayden Road is named for the Wilford Hayden family, pictured here in a Sunday school group shot.

SETTING UP NEW MORTUARY IN 1958 WAS A FAMILY AFFAIR

Scottsdale Republic, August 22, 2008

Our original Scottsdale mortuary was incorporated in September 1958. It was a genuine family affair involving several Scottsdale locals whose help was essential.

My wife, Cora, and I had worked for that day for a long time. My parents gave us some of their dairy pasture in exchange for stock in our new adventure. As such, failure wasn't an option!

We planned to remodel my folk's farmhouse and add a chapel along its south side. We talked with several banks about obtaining a loan. They said Scottsdale was too small to support a mortuary and turned us down.

Then, we went to First Federal Savings and Loan and met Joseph Rice, Sr. A tireless Scottsdale promoter, he believed in our vision and insisted we build what he termed a "first-class" mortuary, one every bit as good as the best found in Phoenix.

There was one small catch. First Federal Savings and Loan was chartered to lend money to build new homes or to businesses involving new home construction. Our plan met neither requirement.

The solution? We decided to build a brand new home on the site and attach our new mortuary to it. He provided 100 percent financing for both buildings.

We built a 6,000-square-foot mortuary with a 1,200-square-foot home attached to it. The new buildings encompassed my folk's original adobe house (which still stands on the southeast corner of Miller and Indian School Roads). Cora and I moved into the newly built house and lived there for the next 31years, operating our mortuary and Scottsdale's first ambulance business from the site.

Getting the home and mortuary funded and built was only one of our challenges. We also had to furnish the mortuary and purchase the vehicles, equipment, caskets and supplies.

We had almost $30,000 of pooled family money in our budget. Since many of the items we needed weren't available in Phoenix, let alone Scottsdale, we traveled to California to purchase our first caskets. They cost about $6,000. We picked up a used funeral coach for $1,600 from Cabot Mortuary in Pasadena.

A 1956 Cadillac limo cost us another $3,200 and a brand new Chevrolet "first call" car cost us $2,250. We also leased a new Buick Cotner/Bevington ambulance for $178 a month. At the time, we were getting $10 for each ambulance call.

Our wool carpets came from Pettyjohn's in Phoenix. They cost $4,200 and lasted 15 years. When our buying spree was over and we opened our doors in 1959, we had about $3,000 left. That's why I continued working in Phoenix until a month before we opened.

John Luke, the manager of the Bank of Douglas, located at Brown and Main Streets in downtown Scottsdale, was another hero in our epic saga. He made me many small loans. I met with him every couple of weeks to either return money to him or borrow more. He and his bank treated us well. Unfortunately, few if any small businessmen are offered similar working relationships with local banks today.

We've worked hard over these past five decades. Family and friends supported us. Lending institutions and suppliers trusted us. In 2009, we will proudly celebrate 50 years of successful business in Scottsdale!

Building Scottsdale's first mortuary in 1958 required a lot of hard work, an investment of family money and local bankers who were creative and supportive. First Federal Savings and Loan was the primary lender. The Bank of Douglas, located at Brown and Main Streets, handled the small loans that helped Messinger Mortuary at Indian School and Miller thrive and grow.

BOY'S LETTER TO HIS DAD PACKED QUITE A STING

Scottsdale Republic, March 6, 2009

Our family moved to Arizona from Grand Rapids, Michigan in 1942. In the cold northern states, we did not have scorpions. When I encountered them for the first time in Arizona, they were new to me.

Early one Saturday morning in January 1943, while I was riding my newspaper route, my 6-year-old sister Mary was stung by a scorpion. I was 13. My mother, not having the knowledge of how to treat this situation, grabbed Mary and drove her to Southside Hospital in Mesa.

When I finished my newspaper route and got home, my brother Phil told me what had happened. This was big news to a 13-year-old. It was especially big news for a boy whose mother had been asking him to write a letter to his father.

My father was back in Grand Rapids, having returned to his former law practice for six weeks to help support his family. Mom had given Phil and me envelopes addressed to our dad with instructions to write him letters. Armed with the scorpion news and Mom's coaxing still ringing in my mind, I immediately sat down and wrote to my father.

I told him of Mary being stung by the "poisonous" scorpion and about Mom taking her to the hospital. While I was writing this letter, Mom called the house to tell us that Mary was coming along fine. So I added the information to my letter that Mom had called and Mary was "doing as well as could be expected."

I signed and sealed the letter and immediately rode my bike to the Scottsdale Post Office and mailed it. My writing duties were done.

Dad, who was working long days in Grand Rapids, got to his apartment the following Monday night around 10:30 or 11:00. While getting ready for bed, he opened and read my letter. Given his lack of knowledge about scorpions, when he read the words "hospital" and "doing as well as could be expected," he became extremely concerned. He got up, got dressed, drove to his office and called Mom.

It was about midnight there and around 10:00 p.m. here. Long-distance calls were rare, particularly in the middle of the night. Mom could barely remember the incident, but she focused on the subject quickly. My father was relieved, but at the late hour, neither of my parents was amused by what I had written in my letter.

We had many scorpion incidents over the following years. Getting stung in the dairy barn's feed room was the most common. When we turned on the light, the scorpions ran everywhere. Each time we were stung, we put ice on the sting for 30-40 minutes or until it stopped hurting.

Mom and Dad continued to encourage me to write letters, but I could never understand why they always wanted to read them before they were mailed.

Shortly after the Messinger family moved from Michigan to Scottsdale, then six-year-old Mary was stung by a scorpion. Not knowing what to do, Vera Messinger grabbed Mary and took her to Southside Hospital in Mesa. Thirteen-year-old Paul wrote all about the incident with the "poisonous" creature in a letter to his father, who was working in Michigan.

1959

The first Messinger Mortuary opened its doors on May 10, 1959 at 7601 East Indian School Road in Scottsdale. Scottsdale's first mortuary, it was very much a family business. Paul was the licensed funeral director, with his wife Cora working by his side. Paul's parents, William and Vera Messinger, provided the financial backing by subordinating their note for a corner of the family's Scottsdale farm as collateral to secure the loan to start the business.

That original building, and its garden chapel, are still in use today. They have been extensively remodeled and expanded over the past 50 years. The most recent expansion was the addition of a community room in 2007. The community room is used extensively for post-service receptions.

1973

In 1973, Messinger Mortuary and Chapel joined with Guy Stillman, Chester Hansen, A.L. Moore, Larry Melcher, Ralph Sage, Paul and Frank Beer and Oligard Kalina to establish Paradise Memorial Gardens, a cemetery in what was then North Scottsdale on 92nd Street and Shea Boulevard. The first interment took place in 1974. They added Arizona's fifth crematory in 1977.

Messinger Mortuary, Indian School

Paradise Memorial Gardens

1983

In 1983, Messinger Mortuary acquired sole ownership of the cemetery. A mausoleum and columbarium were added in 1992. The mausoleum was extensively expanded in 2008. Today, it serves 2,000 families.

1995

In 1995, Messinger purchased the original Fountain Hills visitors' center which had been built by McCullough Properties and turned it into the community's first funeral home, Messinger Fountain Hills Mortuary. After serving as the community's visitors' center, the building was used as a restaurant and a church before becoming a mortuary.

1999

In 1999, Messinger Mortuary and Chapel purchased the Payson Funeral Home and Mountain Meadow Memorial Park and crematory in Gila County. In 2010, Payson Funeral Home broke ground on a brand new, 14,000 square foot facility on 2 ¼ acres adjacent to the old building. The new building is expected to open in 2011.

2000

In 2000, the beautiful Messinger Pinnacle Peak Mortuary opened in North Scottsdale, near Pinnacle Peak and Pima roads. It features a community room that is used for community functions, voting and post-service receptions.

2009

In 2009, Messinger celebrated 50 years of dedicated service to Arizona families.

Messinger Mortuary, Fountain Hills

Messinger Mortuary, Pinnacle Peak

Under the guidance of the Messinger family and some wonderful, longtime staff, the firm has established a rich legacy of service to the communities of Scottsdale, Fountain Hills and Payson. The successful development of the mortuaries, cemeteries and crematories would not have been possible without the extensive commitment by dedicated and experienced staffers who make a difference in the lives of all the people they serve. The Messinger Mortuaries staff has the tools, and the support of the ownership, to continue providing professional, empathetic care. It is the people at all the Messinger Mortuaries facilities who continue to provide comfort to families generation after generation.

A PROFILE OF THE AUTHOR, PAUL MESSINGER

By Lois McFarland

At age 81, Scottsdale businessman and community leader Paul Messinger has no plans to retire. In fact, still thinking like the farm boy who got up before school to milk the cows, he puts in a 10-hour day seven days a week and is on call 24/7 as president of Messinger Mortuaries.

"My health and the good Lord will help decide when it's time to retire," he said.

The Messinger Mortuary and Chapel opened its doors a half-century ago on Mother's Day, May 10, 1959, at 7601 E. Indian School Road, making it one of the city's longest operating businesses.

Paul and his wife, Cora Ross, were married on Thanksgiving Day, Nov. 23, 1950 in Coolidge. That was the only place they could find a Justice of the Peace willing to marry them on the holiday more than 60 years ago.

A native of Grand Rapids, Michigan, Paul came to Scottsdale with his parents in 1942. He and his younger brother and sister helped with chores on the family's 10-acre dairy, chicken, turkey, alfalfa and melon farm at the southeast corner of Indian School and Miller roads. This is the same site where years later he established the first Messinger Mortuary.

Paul has been active in his community. He served as City Councilman from 1971-76, followed by three terms in the Arizona House of Representatives from 1979-85. During his council years, the Indian Bend Wash Greenbelt was established. McCormick Ranch, the city's first planned community, was planned and built. The Scottsdale Center for the Arts opened, and Scottsdale Municipal Airport was developed from Thunderbird Field, a World War II flight school, into a municipal airport.

He chaired the STEP Committee that brought Scottsdale Community College to Scottsdale (1967-70) and was on the citizen's committee that helped locate the Scottsdale City Hall and the Scottsdale Main Library on their present sites in 1965.

While in the Legislature, Paul worked on the Groundwater Act of 1980. In 1982, he worked to pass the Constitutional Act that restricts budgets of government entities and introduced legislation that saved the old Carnegie Library building in downtown Phoenix.

A champion of historic preservation and Western art, Paul chaired the grassroots fundraising for The Yearlings bronze sculpture at the entrance to the Civic Center Mall and worked on the One with the Eagle at the entrance to the Scottsdale Airpark. Since 1980, his efforts have focused on bringing a Museum of the West to Scottsdale.

Paul is a life member of the Scottsdale Charros and led the group as "Patron" in 1969. He served three terms on the Scottsdale Chamber of Commerce board and is a past president of the Scottsdale Western Art Association.

His work in the funeral industry is well documented. He is a past president of the Arizona Funeral Directors Association, past president of the Arizona State Board of Funeral Directors and Embalmers and longtime board member of the National Selected Morticians Association.

Index

ACKNOWLEDGEMENTS

Scottsdale Memories is a sampling of 50 columns that originally appeared as a bi-weekly feature in the Scottsdale Republic between 2004 and 2009. Joanie Flatt of Flatt & Associates, Ltd., Public Relations and Public Affairs, encouraged me to write the columns as a way to capture my memories of Scottsdale, the Valley of the Sun and family remembrances going back to when I was a boy growing up in this area in the 1940s.

I am deeply grateful to Joanie's late colleague, Dan Durrenberger, for serving as my original editor. Since Dan's passing in 2009, Joanie has taken on those editorial duties and served as my editor for this book.

I want to thank the very talented Louis Giordano for handling all the design duties for the book. Thanks also to Paula Beavin of Flatt & Associates for serving as our ever-efficient editorial assistant on the project, and to Connie Forney and the professional team at O'Neil Printing for the excellent job they did on the production of the book.

As has been the case in all that I've done for more than 60 years, my wife, Cora, contributed to this project. She assisted me with research, suggested column ideas, provided input on our selection of photos and encouragement. Thank you, Cora.

The Scottsdale Memories columns, which I continue to write on a bi-weekly basis, would not have been possible without a wide circle of friends who have always been there to help with ideas, dates, names, memories and general research. These are the people I have turned to many times over the years for assistance, and they have always been there for me. Some of these dear friends have already passed on, but I want their families to know how much I appreciate them.

Thank you Burl Avery, Doc Cavalliere, Carl Cluff, Esperanza Dominguez, Joyce Eller, Joan Fudala, JoAnne Hanley, Helen Hughes, Sue and Bill Jenkins, Lois McFarland, Labuella Mowry, Jean Shipp, John Song, Marshall Trimble, Patricia Underhill and Sue Witzeman.

Thanks also to our staff at Messinger Mortuaries, cemeteries and crematories for your many story ideas and the numerous times you covered for me when I needed time to work on a column.

Finally, I want to thank the Scottsdale Republic, and Editorial Page Editor Robert Leger, for continuing to bring my Scottsdale Memories reminiscences to Northeast Valley readers. I continue to enjoy telling the stories from our community's history.